T0318994

Cambridge Elements ≡

Elements in Public and Nonprofit Administration
edited by
Andrew Whitford
University of Georgia
Robert Christensen
Brigham Young University

ORGANIZATIONAL OBLIVIOUSNESS

Entrenched Resistance to Gender Integration in the Military

Alesha Doan
University of Kansas

Shannon Portillo
University of Kansas

CAMBRIDGE
UNIVERSITY PRESS

CAMBRIDGE
UNIVERSITY PRESS

University Printing House, Cambridge CB2 8BS, United Kingdom

One Liberty Plaza, 20th Floor, New York, NY 10006, USA

477 Williamstown Road, Port Melbourne, VIC 3207, Australia

314–321, 3rd Floor, Plot 3, Splendor Forum, Jasola District Centre,
New Delhi – 110025, India

79 Anson Road, #06–04/06, Singapore 079906

Cambridge University Press is part of the University of Cambridge.

It furthers the University's mission by disseminating knowledge in the pursuit of
education, learning, and research at the highest international levels of excellence.

www.cambridge.org
Information on this title: www.cambridge.org/9781108465434
DOI: 10.1017/9781108665124

First published 2019

A catalogue record for this publication is available from the British Library.

ISBN 978-1-108-46543-4 Paperback
ISSN 2515-4303 (online)
ISSN 2515-429X (print)

Cambridge University Press has no responsibility for the persistence or accuracy of
URLs for external or third-party internet websites referred to in this publication
and does not guarantee that any content on such websites is, or will remain,
accurate or appropriate.

Organizational Obliviousness

Entrenched Resistance to Gender Integration in the Military

Elements in Public and Nonprofit Administration

DOI: 10.1017/9781108665124
First published online: June 2019

Alesha Doan
University of Kansas

Shannon Portillo
University of Kansas

Author for correspondence: Alesha Doan adoan@ku.edu

Abstract: Exploring efforts to integrate women into combat forces in the military, we investigate how resistance to equity becomes entrenched, ultimately excluding women from being full participants in the workplace. Based on focus groups (N = 198) and surveys (N = 1915) with members of Special Operations, we found most of the resistance is rooted in traditional gender stereotypes that are often bolstered through organizational policies and practices. The subtlety of these practices often renders them invisible. We refer to this invisibility as *organizational obliviousness*. Obliviousness exists at the individual level; it becomes reinforced at the cultural level; and, in turn, cultural practices are entrenched institutionally by policies. Organizational obliviousness may not be malicious or done to actively exclude or harm, but the end result is that it does both. Throughout this Element, we trace the ways that organizational obliviousness shapes individuals, culture, and institutional practices throughout the organization.

Keywords: organizational obliviousness, gender integration, policies and practices, military, Special Forces

ISBNs: 9781108465434 (PB) 9781108665124 (OC)
ISSNs: 2515-4303 (online) 2515-429X (print)

Contents

1 Introduction

> Our job is to get the mission done and come back alive. Unless you've been in this environment or been deployed you cannot understand. Females are not as capable in dealing with the physical and emotional demands of Special Forces. Listen to the people who are here and don't just make that decision based on, "America wants women to be integrated everywhere." Well that's nice. It's a good conversation over the dinner table. Take that overseas where your life's on the line. And that's why I will leave if they do not listen to us, the guys on the teams. I'm telling you [integration] does not work.
>
> (John, Participant)

Resistance to organizational change is commonplace and has traditionally been conceptualized as resistance from workers to managerial initiatives that challenge the status quo of the organization (Piderit 2000). However, this view has largely been critiqued as ahistorical and lacking a nuanced understanding of organizational context (Kuipers et al., 2014; Pettrigrew et al., 2001). Moreover, several questions remain unanswered regarding the causes of resistance to organizational change (Kuipers et al., 2014). While there are certainly overt, specific ways that organizations and some individuals working within them attempt to keep women out of traditionally male-occupied professions, many of the contemporary obstacles to women's success are invisible and under-examined within this literature. Although some resistance is easily identifiable, other forms blend into the culture of the organization, making it difficult to pinpoint. The gendered nature of norms, practices, and policies within male-dominated organizations is rarely visible to the people who perpetuate them. However, they collectively become embedded in the organizational culture, which takes on an assumed naturalness or rightness that makes gendered practices hard to see.

We refer to this as *organizational obliviousness*, which calls attention to the intangible ways that stereotypes influence the everyday practices of the individual and organization. The power of organizational obliviousness, as an element of organizational resistance, lies in its covert nature. Obliviousness resides at the individual level; when most organizational actors with similar beliefs confirm it, it becomes reinforced at the cultural level. In turn, cultural practices are further entrenched at the institutional level by policies and norms. Unlike covert forms of resistance, organizational obliviousness is typically neither malicious nor intentional. It operates off norms and stereotypes built into society, culture, and organizations. Nonetheless, organizational obliviousness operates alongside covert resistance, which results in establishing and maintaining systemic discrimination and workplace inequity, making reform complicated. Our research looks to uncover patterns of practice perpetuated by people in the organization that materialize into entrenched resistance to organizational change. While organizational obliviousness as a concept may apply to a variety of stereotypes based on race, gender, and other identity factors, here we focus on the recent resistance to gender integration in the military, specifically within Special Forces (SF).

John, like most of the male participants in our research, opposed gender integration. He was oblivious to the stereotypes he invoked about women and unaware of the subtle way he confirmed these stereotypes at the cultural level of the organization by claiming that all seasoned male soldiers know that integrating women is doomed. Lacking evidence to support his argument, John nonetheless believes that his voice as an experienced insider – and the voices of his male colleagues – should be the authoritative voice on the issue rather than leaving the decision to leaders or elected officials or evolving the organization to accommodate changing societal norms. John raises a compelling argument that soldiers' experiences should factor into the decision. However, in articulating this argument, John is oblivious to the reality that women have been prohibited from serving in SF; therefore, by virtue of policy, women could never weigh in as an authoritative voice about gender integration.

Organizational obliviousness is another component of resistance that creates barriers to equity that ultimately limit people with marginalized identities from being full participants in the workplace. John's quote captures the key tenets of this concept. He draws on gender stereotypes, confirms them at the cultural level of the organization, and does not recognize the tangible ways his organization has restricted the professional roles available for women. When John references "our job" and suggests that unless you have "been deployed" a person cannot relate to the work, he insinuates that the job and deployments are exclusively male activities and depicts an organization devoid of women. He even suggests the prospect of gender integration making "good" dinner conversation, indicating that this hypothetical situation is thought provoking and somewhat entertaining. John's comments omit women as active subjects in the military and illuminate the unnoticed ways resistance to gender equity becomes woven into the fabric of an organization.

Although John erases women's contributions, women have participated in every major military conflict in US history. Historical data documents that women have informally been a part of the US military since the Revolutionary War (Skaine, 1999), but they were unable to formally enlist until World War I (Devilbiss, 1990). At the end of World War II, the Women's Armed Service Integration Act of 1948 was the first policy to permanently recognize women's service to the military. Under this policy, women could serve but were barred from combat, not allowed to hold a rank higher than lieutenant colonel, and were prohibited from having command over a man (Morden, 1990). Over time, some of these policies were revised to reflect changing gender norms in the military workplace, and others were further delineated. In 1994, the Department of Defense (DoD) enacted the Direct Ground Combat Exclusion Policy, which formally codified women's exclusion from combat positions in the military (Burrelli, 2013).

More recently, military leaders, politicians, and civilians have claimed that the U.S. Combat Exclusion Policy is at odds with the de facto reality that women are already engaged in direct combat (MacKenzie, 2015; Keenan, 2008). Addressing this contemporary state, the Military Leadership Diversity Commission released a report that recommended removal of the combat exclusion policy. By January 2013, then Secretary of Defense Leon Panetta announced the DoD was rescinding the policy and would begin to create gender-neutral occupational performance standards for all positions. Nearly all combat positions in the military were opened to women effective January 2016. Currently, the combat exclusion policy has changed, and military leaders are working to integrate positions in practice.

Even though the current policy has the potential to disrupt the masculine identity of the military writ large, the findings of our research, which come from original surveys and focus groups, indicate that persistent and pervasive patterns of inequality exist and remain unchallenged in the workplace. The male participants of our research are members of Special Forces, which is an elite component of Army Special Operations Command. Female participants come from other units within Army Special Operations Command. Our research locates most of this inequality in the traditional gender stereotypes ascribed to by most military members in our study. *Gender stereotypes* refer to the assumed emotional and physical differences between men and women as groups that are inappropriately applied to individuals. The systemic impact of gendered beliefs is masked in the context of the institution even though stereotypes are infused throughout cultural norms and organizational practices and policies.

1.1 Gendered Organizational Structures

Our research, which we place in conversation with the gendered organization literature, is not the first to recognize the gendered nature of practices and policies within the workplace (Acker, 1990). Workplace organizations are often thought to have distinctive identities, and the military is no exception (MacKenzie, 2015). *Organizational identities* are the statements of values that members perceive to be central and enduring to the organization (Albert & Whetten, 1985). Scholars once argued that organizational identities were fixed (e.g., Albert & Whetten, 1985). However, there is now a robust scholarly conversation documenting how organizational identity shifts based on insider and outsider perceptions (Gioia et al., 2000) and the institutional and political contexts of the organization (Powell & DiMaggio, 2012). Gioia and colleagues (2000) argue that organizational identity is fraught with continual negotiation that leads to incremental change. This type of identity instability allows organizations to adapt to changing conditions in their environment and the military is not an exception.

Long recognized as a masculine organization, the military has not been immune from evolving political contexts and organizational demographic changes. Since 1973, the percentage of women serving in the military among enlisted ranks has increased sevenfold from 2 percent to 14 percent, and among officers, women's share has quadrupled – rising from 4 percent to 16 percent (Patten & Parker, 2011). However, the influx of female soldiers into the US armed forces has done little to quell the gendered culture of the military or alter expected gender roles within the institution (MacKenzie, 2015). Even as more women enter the military, Enloe (2000) argues the military's emphasis on gender differences is used to keep women in subordinate positions and maintain hegemonic masculinity as a central aspect of the military's identity. Familiar gender tropes often frame contemporary resistance to full integration and accentuate the social construction of men as "protectors" and women as "needing protection." These gendered constructions have continued to underscore men's position as belonging in the public sphere while relegating women to the private sphere (Elshtain, 1995). The military is not alone or unique in its ongoing struggle to diversify and become a more inclusive work environment. Resistance to gender integration has been commonly documented in many traditionally male-dominated organizations, such as policing (Prokos & Padavic, 2002; Martin & Jurik, 1996) and firefighting (Hulett et al., 2008). Beyond these traditionally male-dominated organizations, gendered practices and processes are also pervasive in other institutions including local government administration (Voorhees & Lange-Skaggs, 2015). As we discuss in detail in the ensuing sections, many of the subtly gendered practices operating at the micro and macro-levels that hold women back in careers outside of the military were also present in our exploration of gender integration in SF.

While much of the micro-level research of organizational identity focuses on the views of individuals both internal and external to the organization, there is also a robust discussion of organizational structures and macro-level issues. Organizations, in addition to individuals, may be gendered. A growing collection of scholars has argued that perceiving organizational structures as a neutral space is flawed and ignores the underlying assumptions regarding gender, race, socioeconomic status, and sexual orientation that permeate the documents, contracts, policies, and practices used to create and maintain organizations (Acker, 2006, 1990; Britton, 2000). The imagined worker in this "neutral" organization is a middle-class, middle-aged, white male. Yet, scholars contend that policies and practices, while gender-neutral on their face, are built around deeply embedded assumptions regarding gender (and other sociodemographic characteristics). This "gendered organizational logic" (Acker, 2006, 1990; Britton, 2000, 1997) reinforces social hierarchies outside and within the organization, recreating inequality regimes that live through the structured policies and practices of the organization, rather than through individual perceptions alone.

The concept of "gendered organizations" comes from Acker's seminal 1990 work, where she argues that organizational structures are not gender-neutral and that these gendered structures shape the culture and outcomes of organizations. Building on Acker's (1990) foundational work, Britton (2000) argues for more theoretical specificity in how we consider the concept of "gendered organizations" in our scholarship. She examines three theoretical strands of this concept. The first, most closely related to Acker's original work, argues that ideal-type bureaucratic organizations are inherently gendered; they have been defined, conceived, and structured with a masculine or feminine distinction and will thus reproduce these differences and advantages. The second is less theoretically grounded and largely focuses on the occupational level, arguing that occupations are gendered to the extent that one sex – male or female – dominates them. The third does not distinguish between the organizational and occupational levels, arguing that gendered discourse rooted in masculine hegemony reinforces gendered hierarchies advancing masculine notions of good leadership and management at the organizational and professional levels.

"The Schoolhouse," as it is known in the Special Operations community, at Ft. Bragg, North Carolina, exemplifies gendered organizational logic. Designated as a space to train Special Operations soldiers, the Schoolhouse was originally established with male-only barracks and restrooms. More recently, facilities have been installed to accommodate women when they are training at the Schoolhouse, but they are located a farther distance than the men's facilities. Consequently, women take longer to complete their hygiene needs in the morning and during breaks because they must travel farther to access facilities. At the Schoolhouse, women are attempting to fit into an environment that was designed with men in mind, and they try hard not to draw attention to the inadequacies of their accommodations. Even though the actual time to complete hygiene tasks is similar for men and women, on the surface it appears that women require more time, which reinforces the stereotype that women need the extra time for "primping" for the day. This physical layout creates a space that disadvantages women and reinforces gender stereotypes, but this arrangement is not unique to the military. Plaskow (2008) notes that the lack of women's bathrooms in public space had everything to do with restricting women's movements and establishing who is welcomed into a profession. Using Congress as an example, there was not a women's bathroom near the Senate floor until 1993 or near the House of Representatives floor until 2011. Plaskow notes that the lack of bathrooms for women "function[s] as an explicit argument against hiring women or admitting them into previously all-male organizations" (pp. 52–3). If there are no "facilities" for women, organizations can draw on this history and make a case for excluding women, or other marginalized groups, because the physical space of the institution is not conducive to accommodating them.

Bathrooms function as a way to control access. Those who do not have easy access to the facilities are unable to fully participate. The need to travel to a faraway designated bathroom in the workplace, as women working in Congress did up until 2011, takes a toll on the women who are performing what becomes invisible, extra labor that adversely affects them. This labor was made visible during the 2016 presidential primary when Hillary Clinton was widely criticized for returning late from a commercial break during a televised debate. While some pundits quickly started speculating about her health or her commitment as a candidate, others noted the gendered nature of restroom accommodations at the debate facilities (Chemaly, 2015; Linskey, 2015). There were fewer women's restrooms, and they were farther away from the stage. Secretary Clinton had to travel a greater distance during the break than her male rivals to accomplish the same task. She was criticized for returning later than the men in the debate, but few noted that the physical structure of the venue was created for the convenience of male leaders on stage.

In research focused on women working in traditionally male-dominated organizations, Britton (2003, 1997) points out that it is not just the physical infrastructure that reinforces gendered organizations. She emphasizes that training for correctional officers defines the ideal officer as possessing a particular type of hegemonic masculinity; therefore, male recruits often appear more prepared and normatively in line with the efforts of the organization. While masculinity is not directly tied to the functions of the work, it is infused in the concept of the ideal worker. When women in these organizations perform well, they are often stereotyped by colleagues as masculine, with the assumption that their success has to do with their proximity to the male ideal rather than their ability to perform the gender-neutral tasks of the work (Jurik, 1988, 1985; Owen & Dennis, 1988; Zimmer, 1988). Connell (2006) criticizes the efforts of organizational reformers pushing for a gender-neutral understanding of work, noting that it is important to recognize the role gender does play within agencies.

The push to make gender-neutral workplaces may obfuscate what Kanter (1977) refers to as the tokenizing role that gender has in shaping organizational circumstances and the traditionally gendered divisions of labor. In her classic work on women in the corporate world, Kanter (1977) discussed tokenism, where a woman's presence (or that of a member of an underrepresented group) is highlighted by an organization to convey diversity and access to equal employment opportunities, when in practice the organization is using her presence to gloss over its lack of diversity and equality. Tokenism continues to be relevant in contemporary times, leading to different outcomes for minoritized employees. Kantar and other scholars argue that an individual can benefit from being tokenized because they may gain resources or attention, but overall, being tokenized is detrimental to the progress of women in the organization because it masks their limited numbers (Fuegen & Biernart, 2002; Goldenhar et al., 1998). Similarly, Lewis and Simpson (2012, 2010) argue that gendered dynamics are continually acted out within organizations; therefore, they must be made visible within organizations to study their effects and actively work toward reform.

Kanter (2008, 1977) presents the solution as a simple numbers game, contending that as more women enter an organization, they will acquire greater power that will ultimately level the playing field. However, the empirical evidence supporting this solution is mixed. While some studies in public organizations have found that increasing the number of women in leadership positions within an organization is a necessary precondition for altering gender-based power imbalances, other studies have concluded that female leadership has little impact (Saidel & Loscocco 2005; Kaiser et al., 2002; Dolan 2000). In addition, several critics have pushed back on Kanter's (1977) numbers-based solution, arguing that gender disadvantage is also infused in the structure of organizations, which reinforces the existing power dynamics (Lewis & Simpson, 2012; Zimmer, 1988). Gaining numbers is not the same as gaining power within organizations; therefore, relying on gender-neutral concepts is not a panacea for solving inequity (Zimmer, 1988). Rather, Lewis and Simpson (2010, 2012) argue that scholars must unearth the ways in which gender shapes the policies and practices of organizations. Seeing equity as a moral imperative, Connell (2006) asserts that public organizations have an obligation to excavate and reform gendered practices in an effort to move away from resistance to more equitable workplaces.

There are two broad conceptualizations of organizational resistance. The first comes from public management scholarship and the second from organizational culture scholarship. In the public management literature, organizational resistance has been used to describe both organizational-level actions and traits that create barriers to change (Jurik, 1985). Much of this literature focuses on the structural aspects of organizations; however, Kumar and Kant (2006) argue that organizational resistance to change can be described on two levels: "structural" and "cultural." Organizational culture is composed of the beliefs and expectations that "produce norms or commitments – informal rules for behavior – that provide a context which individuals in an organization can interpret and approach their work" (Kumar & Kant, 2006, p. 148). Dull (2010) writes, "Public sector leaders attempt to cultivate organizational culture as a means of controlling administrative behavior and building organizational competence, defined as the skill and capacity to accomplish necessary tasks" (p. 858). From this perspective, effective performance follows an established culture. A primary characteristic of organizational culture is its resistance to change (Dull, 2010; Schein, 2010). Gagliardi (1986) notes, "When new strategies assume the presence of new values that are antagonistic towards traditional ones, there is very little chance of them ever being carried through" (p. 129). Adding to the challenges, Schein (2010) contends that organizational members resist change because their culture tells them "who they are, how to behave toward each other, and how to feel good about themselves" (p. 29). Changing organizational culture can produce significant anxiety among members because it erodes the assumptions they have been using to derive comfort and understanding about themselves (Schein, 2010, 1990).

The underlying anxiety that fuels much of the organizational resistance to women in the military is not unique to this institution. Recently, much of the discussion around inequality in organizations has focused on unconscious or implicit bias, which refers to the broad underlying stereotypes that often animate decision making (Jolls & Sunstein, 2006). Research findings on unconscious and implicit bias have consistently demonstrated that traditionally marginalized groups uniquely face subtle barriers in many workplaces because people routinely rely on heuristics or mental shortcuts that are foregrounded in stereotypes (Jolls & Sunstein, 2006). Specific to racism, Bonilla-Silva and Dietrich (2011) refer to this process as color-blind racism to capture the "unacknowledged, contextual standpoints that provide the intellectual (and moral) building blocks whites use to explain racial matters" (p. 192). Since people are largely unaware of their biases, or the ways in which they are relying on standard social scripts, they rarely work to overcome unconscious bias despite its influence on individual decision making (Bonilla-Silva, 2006; Jolls & Sunstein, 2006). Gender bias operates in a similar manner.

Once people use gender as a cue for a social script, it is hard to undo, even in workplace settings where other identity factors may be more salient (Ridgeway, 1997). Ridgeway (1997) refers to many of these intangible obstacles that women face as the "interactional gender mechanisms that operate as the 'invisible hand'" reinforcing gender hierarchies within the workplace (p. 218). Ridgway goes on to argue that these gendered status beliefs are structural within the workplace. Institutional practices, like job evaluations and internal labor markets, incorporate gendered assumptions and stereotypes. Even as organizations open to women, these assumptions and status beliefs persist through organizational inertia. Organizational politics also come into play as men attempt to maintain their advantages through overt and covert practices. Leadership is often male-dominated with male views represented in decision making and subtle biases rarely called out in spaces of organizational leadership. Sex-based stereotypes and occupational sex segregation become increasingly normalized even when gender is irrelevant to the functions of the job. The "invisible hand" of gender biases results in men regularly acting in their own self-interests, even if unintentionally. This behavior results in differential outcomes for men and women.

Placing the gendered organizational literature and unconscious bias scholarship in conversation suggests that individual legal cases and specific policy change will not be enough to reform male-dominated organizations. Our research begins to bridge these literatures using empirical data that originates from an organizational insider perspective that provides a fertile entry point for identifying the individual gendered beliefs and day-to-day practices that maintain organizational resistance to change and an inequitable work environment (Lewis & Simpson, 2010). Throughout the Element, we introduce stories and flesh out the nuances of organizational obliviousness, relying on in-depth qualitative data from focus groups with active duty soldiers and two surveys administered to active duty men serving in SF and women serving in Special Operations. We find that individuals rely on stereotypes and heuristic shortcuts, often without malice, but their actions lead to systematic errors that reinforce other institutionalized forms of discrimination in the workplace (Jolls & Sunstein, 2006). As we argue throughout this Element, organizational obliviousness to gender inequality exists – and must be intentionally confronted – on multiple levels within an organization.

1.2 Research Design and Background

Our data comes from a grant-funded project examining soldiers' perspectives regarding the potential barriers and benefits of integrating women into Special Forces, which served two research purposes. The first purpose and more immediate aspect of the project was providing high-ranking US Army personnel with an assessment of the range and severity of the barriers that could potentially impede gender integration. The second purpose and longer-term aspect of this project was using the US Army as a site for conducting exploratory research on gender and organizations. We used a sequential mixed methods design composed of focus groups that were in turn used to design two surveys eliciting soldiers' opinions regarding the potential barriers and benefits of integrating women into SF (Hesse-Biber, 2015). Given the lack of data available on the topic, we were interested in developing theory from soldiers' lived experiences and exploring how these experiences have shaped their beliefs about gender integration using grounded theory (Charmaz, 2006). This methodology provided us with flexibility to pursue unanticipated topics that surfaced during the focus groups and include them in subsequent groups, and ultimately our survey design (Charmaz, 2006).

1.2.1 Background

SF, commonly known as the Green Berets, are an exclusive unit of Army Special Operations Command. Fewer than 10 percent of the men who apply to become a Green Beret end up making it through screening and assessment. SF teams are regularly deployed in small-person units called Operational Detachment Alpha (ODA). When deployed, SF operators often closely rely on one another, with no forward operating base or support teams to fall back on. Even when they are training and stateside, most ODAs spend significant on-duty and off-duty time together.

Female participants in our study came from Civilian Affairs (CA), Military Information Support Operations (MISO), and Cultural Support Teams (CSTs) – all units within Army Special Operations. Each of these units serves as support for SF when they are deployed. CA and MISO are long-standing units that are gender integrated. CA focuses on engaging with local populations and building strategic connections with local leaders, whereas MISO focuses on intelligence gathering and analysis. CST is a newer unit, developed in response to current military conflicts. CSTs are exclusively female and recruited to deploy with SF units specifically to interact with women and children in Iraq and Afghanistan.

1.2.2 Research Design

Our data was collected in 2013 and 2014 after the ground combat exclusion policy was rescinded, but when Special Operations was still considering asking for an exception. We conducted twenty-seven focus groups, with a nonrandom sample of 198 participants at multi-day site visits at five military bases. Twenty-three focus groups consisted of men and four focus groups consisted of women. Our professional position as military outsiders who lacked a preconceived agenda regarding military policies was advantageous for building rapport with participants. We followed a semi-structured script asking participants general questions about their military experience, potential obstacles and benefits to gender integration, experiences working with people of the other sex, and experiences while deployed overseas. All focus groups lasted approximately two hours.

The SF community is small, generally older, and less racially diverse compared to the broader army. Consequently, we were sensitive about collecting information from participants that could easily identify them. We intentionally refrained from asking participants about their race or other demographic information; however, on occasion, a participant shared this information while relaying an opinion or longer story. Pseudonyms are used for all participants, and we obtained human subjects' approval for this research. In designing the focus groups, we were sensitive to workplace hierarchy and tried to create groups that would foster uncensored opinions. To reduce potential power dynamics, in twenty-one of the focus groups we divided participants by rank with enlisted soldiers, warrant officers, and commissioned officers in separate groups. We also conducted three focus groups with full ODAs, which gave us an opportunity to observe how participants articulated, discussed, and at times revised their opinions among trusted members of their small group. The four focus groups conducted with female soldiers occurred after the male focus groups concluded, which was a function of logistics rather than design. These groups were configured differently due to the limited numbers of women serving in Special Operations; they contained a mix of enlisted soldiers and commissioned officers. All the focus groups were recorded, transcribed verbatim, and analyzed. The results of the analysis were then used to develop two comprehensive surveys. Surveys were used as an additional source of data that provided a more systematic perspective of soldiers' opinions about the barriers and benefits of gender integration in Special Forces, which complemented the nonrandom sample of the focus groups. These surveys were largely identical with some questions on each specific to the target group of respondents.

Initial analysis of focus group transcripts included a line-by-line reading to develop emergent themes by coding words or phrases in vivo (using the words of our participants) whenever possible (Charmaz, 2006). Next, we reread and recoded with more focused codes using taxonomic analysis as a path to data synthesis. Ultimately, we coded fifty-seven unique variables that developed in vivo from the initial analysis. We treated each change in speaker as a new observation, which produced 15,227 observations. Following Charmaz (2006), ours was an iterative and multiphased approach.

Our inductive analysis of the focus groups was then balanced with systematic data collected from our surveys. The first survey was designed for all Active Duty and National Guard SF men; the population of US SF men is 6,109. The second survey was designed for CA and MISO women and CST female enablers currently assigned to US Army Special Operations Command (N = 779). The surveys were administered online in the spring of 2014. Each respondent took approximately fifteen minutes to complete the survey. In total, the surveys yielded a sample size of 1,613 active duty men and 88 National Guard men (27.8 percent response rate) as well as 214 active duty women (27.6 percent response rate).

The mean age of female survey respondents was 32 (ages ranged from 20–50 with a median of 31) and 37 for men (ages ranged from 24–55 with a median of 35). Most male respondents identified as White ($n = 1,116$, 80 percent), 7 percent ($n = 99$) identified as Black, 3 percent ($n = 46$) identified as Asian American, 3 percent ($n = 46$) identified as "other," and 6 percent ($n = 93$) responded they "don't know." Two-thirds of female respondents ($n = 131$, 64 percent) identified as White, 15 percent ($n = 31$) identified as Black, 11 percent ($n = 22$) identified as Asian American, 5 percent ($n = 10$) identified as "other," and 6 percent ($n = 12$) responded "don't know." Marriage and parenthood rates varied considerably across men and women. Seventy-eight percent ($n = 1,083$) of men were married and 75 percent ($n = 1,049$) had children. For women, 45 percent ($n = 88$) were married and 44 percent ($n = 86$) had children.

In terms of work experience, the survey population had longer work experience compared to the general enlisted army population. Almost half (47 percent, $n = 98$) of female survey respondents had served in the military nine or more years (range = 0–25+ years); for male respondents this number was 78 percent ($n = 1,287$ with a range of 0–25+ years). In addition, the clear majority of survey respondents had served in a combat zone (95 percent of men, $n = 1,569$ and 94 percent of women, $n = 166$). The survey respondents were also highly educated. Twenty-six percent of women ($n = 50$) were college graduates, and an additional 33 percent ($n = 64$) had some postgraduate education. For the men, 29 percent ($n = 404$) were college graduates and another 12 percent ($n = 168$) had postgraduate education.

Grounded in the data from these surveys and focus groups, in the following sections we examine how organizational resistance to gender integration manifests and includes organizational obliviousness. In Section 2, we explore how gender hierarchies are reinforced through the pervasive invocation of gender stereotypes, which are embraced by men and women. Following our discussion of organizational obliviousness at the individual level, in Section 3 we explore how these individual beliefs become plaited into the culture of the organization. Finally, in Section 4 we explore how gender stereotyping works in tandem with formal policies to systematically structure an inequitable work environment that is subtly sustained through a pattern of organizational obliviousness and broader organizational resistance to change.

2 Entrenched Resistance at the Individual Level

> It depends on the woman wholeheartedly. But, in my opinion, you can't push a female as hard because they get more emotional. Then they take it more personally. Whereas if you look at somebody and tell them, hey you've f–ed up, you can be friends in five minutes. It doesn't seem like it works that way when you're dealing with the different sexes interacting.
>
> (Steven, Participant)

In this section, we explore how organizational obliviousness is foregrounded in the social construction of gender. Resistance to gender equity manifests through individual men and women who, like Steven, reinforce hierarchies by drawing on familiar gendered stereotypes to frame their opposition to integration. Throughout the focus groups, biologically and emotionally rooted stereotyping frequently framed the conversation in contradictory and complex ways. Men overwhelmingly relied on quintessential, binary constructions of gender and sexuality, navigating between stereotyping themselves in positive, masculine terms and women in negative, feminine terms. Unlike their male colleagues, women infrequently drew on male stereotypes, but they were just as likely to negatively stereotype other women while holding themselves apart as atypical, or as Steven noted, the exception to the rule.

During our focus group discussion, Steven initially presented himself as someone in favor of gender integration in SF, if the women integrating meet the same standards as men in the same positions. However, as Steven continued to talk, he began to make a distinction between an exceptional woman and women as a group. Relying on a traditional stereotype of female hyper-emotionality, Steven identified women's inability to delineate between personal and professional criticism as one reason they were difficult to work with, whereas "somebody," whom he implied is male, can quickly recover and "be friends in five minutes." Steven's remarks underlined his lack of awareness of the well-worn stereotype he was using to describe his female colleagues, while assuming "somebody" and "a person" were men. Steven was not alone in his construction and use of gender stereotypes in the workplace, or his obliviousness to their impact on his colleagues.

Participants in the focus groups continually reinforced and normalized stereotypes that were often constructed from their limited personal experiences and had the effect of defining gender in static and definitive terms. Despite the anecdotal origin of these stereotypes, participants frequently generalized, seeing gender as a factor that affects all people the same way. Men and women were often oblivious to the way they constructed gender in finite and individualistic terms divorced from the larger organizational context where gender roles, behaviors, and expectations are also shaped by cultural norms and expectations.

2.1 Social Construction of Gender

Scholars have long challenged the notion that observed differences between men and women expressed in traits such as aspirations, talents, intelligence, or emotional capacity result from their genetic makeup. Feminist scientists and theorists have painstakingly demonstrated that these so-called inherent differences are attributable to culture and environment, where existing social and power structures in society create meaning that changes over time for groups change over time (Asencio, 2002; Fausto-Sterling, 1992; Butler, 1990). Reflecting their cultural origins, several definitions and contradictory understandings of gender exist in society because they vary according to additional aspects of identity such as race, age, class, and sexual orientation. The construction of gender is also intricately related to sexuality: "Masculinity and femininity are both dependent upon and help to shape the meanings of sexuality; likewise, the interpretation of sexuality helps to structure understandings of gender" (Doan & Williams, 2008, pp. 64–5). As Butler (1990, p. ix) succinctly explains, societal understandings about gender and sexuality are "the effect of institutions, practices, discourses with multiple and diffuse points or origin."

Social institutions, including the workplace, make these categories of identity salient and replete with consequences. In many male-dominated organizations, women are held up to demonstrate what masculinity is not; they are in a sense a "foil" used to demonstrate what organizational members are not or should not be (Prokos & Padavic, 2002). Gender stereotypes that reflect prevailing societal stereotypes are easily relied upon to demarcate women as "othered," reinforcing implicit hierarchies within and beyond the organization. Steven's quote demonstrates this process. Steven used women's alleged heightened emotionality and inability to be "pushed hard" as the context in which he could wrap his tepid support for gender integration. This process is not unique to Steven, or the military. Research has consistently found public organizations such as policing, firefighting, and city management have not fared better on many of these measures (Voorhees & Lange-Skaggs, 2015; Hulett et al., 2008; Martin & Jurik, 2007; Prokos & Padavic, 2002). Far from being limited to state bureaucracies, women working in private industries such as STEM fields, tech, financing, and medicine have experienced similar types of gender stereotyping that have stunted their career progression, limiting the number of women in top leadership positions, and resulting in persistent wage inequity at every level (Petersen & Morgan, 1995).

Following a similar pattern seen across many male-dominated professions, military professionals have often embraced gender stereotypes to exclude women from fully participating in significant portions of the organization. Constructing the military in narrowly defined terms of masculinity has been historically beneficial for the organization where recruitment, cooperation, organization citizenship, and performance have been relevant to the mission and success of the military (Courdileone, 2005; Prokos & Padavic, 2002). As MacKenzie (2015) argues, the exclusion of women from combat has "always been about men, not women" and has been "used to reify the all-male combat unit as elite, essential, and exceptional," thus defining the military's identity and ensuring "male supremacy within the institution" (pp. 3–5). Feminist scholars have long dispelled socially constructed gender stereotypes and have compli-cated this dichotomous understanding of gender roles by noting phenomena such as women's participation in non-state political violence (Parashar, 2009; Stack-O'Connor, 2007; Alison, 2004). However, neither this truism nor larger numbers of women working in the military have dampened the emphasis on gender differences. Regardless of these counterarguments, familiar gender and sexuality tropes continue to underscore much of the contemporary resistance to gender integration (Nagel & Feitz, 2007). As Enloe (2000) argues, the military's continued emphasis on gender differences is used to keep women in subordinate positions and maintain hegemonic masculinity as a central aspect of its identity.

2.2 Menstruation/Hygiene, Protection, Mean Girls, and Sexuality

Throughout our data, SF personnel largely embraced a binary understanding of gender that manifested in distinct patterns. As summarized in Table 1, focus group participants introduced gender stereotypes into the discussion on 1,803 occasions, most frequently (639) linking stereotypes about women to menstrua-tion and hygiene, followed by more generic stereotypes about women (364), and combining stereotypes about men and women together in their discussions (323). Although 14.3 percent of the discussions involved participants' challen-ging the validity of the gender stereotypes being discussed, the vast majority (81.4 percent, 1,467) of stereotypes expressed by men and women reified existing biological and emotional gender stereotypes that clustered around

Table 1 Focus groups frequencies: How often did the respondent invoke a gender stereotype during his or her discussion of gender integration?

Response	Total	Male	Female
Invoked female stereotype	364 (20.2%)	197 (16.10%)	167 (28.6%)
Invoked male stereotype	141 (7.8%)	123 (10.0%)	18 (3.0%)
Combined stereotypes of men and women together	323 (18.0%)	238 (19.5%)	85 (14.6%)
Pushed back or challenged stereotype	258 (14.3%)	120 (9.8%)	138 (23.6%)
Discussed women's menstruation/hygiene needs as obstacle to integration	639 (35.4%)	529 (43.6%)	110 (18.7%)
Discussed women's menstruation/fertility as neutral part of life	78 (4.3%)	13 (1.0%)	65 (11.1%)
Total mentions	1,803	1,220	583

four main themes: menstruation/hygiene, protection, mean girls, and sexuality. Participants predominantly intertwined biological and emotional stereotyping, thus reinforcing the discredited gender distinctions that feminists have long challenged. The expression of these types of stereotypes cleaved along gender lines but not always in expected patterns.

2.2.1 Menstruation/Hygiene

Explicit stereotyping occurred when participants anchored perceived differences in men's and women's ability to serve in SF to genetics, as opposed to societal understandings of gender roles. As summarized in Table 1, men most frequently expressed gendered stereotypes while discussing menstruation (43.6 percent), compared to 18.7 percent of mentions by women. Male participants used women's unique embodied experience of menstruation to create a larger platform for framing their opposition to integration.

Trussing together menstruation and hygiene, men foregrounded their arguments in terms of the limitations women's biology would present working in the field. They subsequently attached additional stereotypes about women to their conversations to buttress their opposition to integration. By tying emotional stereotypes of women to menstruation and hygiene, men had cover to present their stereotypes as neutral information founded in biology as opposed to their underlying opposition to integration, and specifically their discomfort with women in general.

Throughout the male focus groups, menstruation was repeatedly referenced to illustrate that women's bodies starkly contrast with the functioning of men's bodies, which, by implication, do not require such attention and are therefore superior in the field. Menstruation was discussed as an added medical "risk" in the field that would require men to carry additional medical supplies for women's needs. Pulling these themes together, Robert explained why women's bodies mark them as unfit for serving in the field:

> I mean [the] potential for yeast infections and everything without being clean. A woman has a menstrual cycle and all that. These are all things that could definitely be complicated in a situation where you are just pretty filthy and you're living in a dirty environment and you have no way to take care of yourself.

Although Robert does not articulate any misgivings about men's hygiene, including their risk for yeast infections, his preoccupation with women's cleanliness reveals his larger unease with the prospect of having women on an SF team. Careful not to couch their opposition in terms of their own discomfort, men situate it in what they perceive as the medical "risks" menstruation and irregular access to hygiene uniquely pose to women.

Men also layered stereotypical tropes about women's emotional instability onto menstruation. Pinning women's mood fluctuations to their menstrual cycle, Patrick explained to the group that all women, regardless of their professional role or rank, are to be avoided while they menstruate: "It's like a rollercoaster with women. One week can be really good and then all of a sudden, it's that time of the month and you can't even be around them. And that's officer and enlisted, in my experience."

Chris also draws on his personal experience to highlight the emotional chaos women introduce to a group while menstruating: "I'm not being a jerk. I mean, hell I've got five sisters, and I've got a wife. I know there's a period there during the month that you're just, what the hell happened to you and who are you?" Mirroring many men in the focus groups, Chris sees his knowledge of women – based on personal relationships with a handful of women – as a source of expertise that he comfortably extrapolates to stereotype all menstruating women as overly sensitive and emotional.

Menstruation was held up by men as a tangible "event," demonstrating women are unfit to serve in SF, and they linked stereotypes about women's behavior to this physiological occurrence. In doing so, men were oblivious to how they were using menstruation as the benchmark for determining who is fit for SF, while reifying stereotypes about women's emotional instability, which follow women anywhere they go. This oblivion provides cover for men to call women's credibility into question if they express any emotion whereas men are permitted to express a range of emotions because their behavior is not linked to stereotypes built on their physiology.

Unlike the men, women predominantly discussed menstruation as a regular part of their lives. Susan summed up the impact menstruation had on her ability to work: "I can handle myself. I've done this since I was sixteen. This is part of my normal life." In contrast to their male colleagues, women did not view menstruation as a hygiene risk that would create additional health problems, compromise their emotional health, or inhibit their ability to perform in the field. Rather than seeing menstruation as an othering experience that differentiated their experiences from those of men for a significant time of the month, it was a normal part of their everyday lives that they were ready to manage in the workplace.

2.2.2 Protection

Stereotyping of men was done by other men (10 percent) and to a lesser extent by women (3 percent). Male stereotypes were most often positive and constructed in juxtaposition to negative stereotypes of women (see Table 1). Positive stereotypes of men were typically moored to their alleged natural instinct to protect women, which they combined with dominant emotional scripts related to men's superior physical strength and their alpha male personalities. According to participants, these attributes enhanced men's ability to make snap decisions in high-stress environments.

Intertwining biological and socially constructed gendered expectations, men frequently made contradictory claims, simultaneously asserting that their treatment and understanding of women's fragility stemmed from men's genetic makeup and upbringing. This was particularly heightened when men constructed their desire to protect women as part of their own biological hardwiring to "protect" those who are weaker. Threading several of these stereotypes together, Stanley commented, "as a man I have a protective instinct over anything smaller, a child and a woman. I'm married; I have a wife. I look at her different. That's nature. I can't change it." Stanley understands himself, and his role in SF, in terms that are completely "natural" based on gender roles framed by physical size, and traditional nuclear family expectations. By equating women to children, Stanley is oblivious to the fact that his infantilization of women undermines their autonomy and potential ability to perform not only on an SF team but also within the institution.

While Stanley references his wife as a touchstone to illustrate men's protective instinct, Randall, after noting he "doesn't mean to sound caveman or chauvinistic," goes a step further and stereotypes all men as protective and all women as seeking male protection: "There's an evolutionary digression when you get into a situation where females almost look for protection from a man. You can't train that. That's genetic." Randall goes on to connect men's protective instinct with traditional nuclear family roles, which he also believes have a genetic base: "The basic instinct is that men and women get married, [have] kids and all that stuff. You can't get away from that. It's genetics." The presence of a woman on an SF team poses a disruption to Randall's heteronormative narrative whereby "genetics" dictate gender roles and life events including marriage and children. He believes that having women on a team will distract men from the objectives of their mission because of men's protective instinct.

Approaching gender from a different angle that highlights physical attributes, Michael interjected a racial analogy into the conversation to further emphasize the biological differences between men and women:

> So, a black man and a white man. Still men. There's nothing genetically different other than the pigment of your skin. There's genetic differences between men and women, bottom line. I was never raised to look down on, or look up to, a black man or protect a black man, as where I was a woman. So, when genetically the same as me, we can move past race issues and be one in the same. We can't when you're not the same.

Muddling physiological differences with cultural expectations, Michael sees his desire to protect women rooted in biology while unknowingly glossing over how his upbringing shaped his behavior toward women.

While far less common, eight women drew the same biologically grounded explanation, characterizing men as "naturally protective." For women like Becca, being treated "as more of a little sister" by her male colleagues has its downside, even getting "in the way" at work. At times men's protective instinct creates tension for Becca that hampers her ability to perform her job, but she has learned to accept that tension because it is ingrained in men's "human nature." Jennifer likewise describes herself as a capable person, but she also understands that sometimes she must "swallow my pride [because] men in our culture and our society are protective of a woman," which she attributes to the "nature" of men. Neither Becca nor Jennifer sees male protection as "a bad thing as long as it doesn't get in the way of the mission." Their perspectives were exceptional among the women, but not harmless. Both women are willing to acquiesce to men's protective instinct if it does not "interfere" in their ability to perform their job. Becca and Jennifer are oblivious to the impossibility of having "authority" and male protection. Positioning themselves and other women as a group that should accept and accommodate men's "protective nature" reinforces and maintains the unequal gender hierarchy at the individual level of the organization.

Accepting men's position in the organization as natural protectors and women as the protected, Becca and Jennifer are what Prokos and Padavic (2002) refer to as the "foil" for the organization, functioning as a counter-example that demonstrates what masculinity is not. But other women viewed male protection differently. Laura relayed an interaction she had with her colleague to challenge Becca's and Jennifer's flawed logic. Defending his role as a protector, Carl explained to Laura that it "is chivalry. It's not wrong. I am always going to want to protect you." Exposing the inequity of Carl's perspective, Laura retorted, "We don't want you to feel that way. We want to feel like equals. You have to trust in us to be able to do [our jobs] ourselves." Laura's comments underscored the unintended consequences of Carl's obliviousness, namely that the role of protector that he and most male participants have carved out is antithetical to gender equality. Stereotyping women as dependent and in need of male protection permanently positions women as submissive to men within the organization.

Men often linked women's physical weakness to more complex emotional stereotypes about women to voice their trepidation about integration. Summing up women's limitations, Eldon candidly admits, "I just don't think psychologically, emotionally, and physically that they are made to endure that hardship." Even among men like Alex, who recognized that some women can handle the physicality of the job, they often undermined women's potential by defaulting to stereotypes about women's weaker emotional constitution:

> What makes an SF operator different than the rest of the army is not our weapons, not even our mission, but it's the guy that's selected because of his mental, physical, and emotional capability. Can some females who have the fitness and the mental fortitude to go out there and pass selection at the standard that's out there, can they do it? I believe there are females that can. I've seen them. Are there things that can be overcome that they can still do hygiene in a certain way that doesn't change the standard? Yes. It can be done. My concern is the emotional aspect.

Martin similarly recognizes that some women "can make it through SF training," but like Alex, he is concerned that women simply don't have the same mental fortitude as men:

> One of my concerns is that in these split-second scenarios where you have to make a decision, you have to make it quick, and you have to act on it. [Women] are indecisive and they're trying to process multiple things, connecting to it emotionally, and then freezing. This is just talking strictly about how men and women think and process information.

Although Alex hasn't witnessed firsthand a woman "freezing" or being "indecisive" in the field, he nonetheless registers his concern. He also presents his speculations as a narrow and neutral read on women that is limited to their ability to "think and process information." Alex's assessment was not unique. Echoing similar concerns, many SF soldiers in our study expressed stereotypes about women's alleged emotionality, and they were oblivious to the impact this had on women. Men's stereotyping of women's decisional incompetence marked them as a liability in the field and trailed them off the field into the organization where women's credibility was often discounted by male colleagues who perceive women's decision making as emotionally driven rather than rationally driven.

2.2.3 Mean Girls

Compared to their male colleagues, women were far more likely to embrace negative stereotypes of other women when they were not anchored to menstruation or hygiene. Among female focus groups, negative stereotyping of women occurred on 167 occasions (28.6 percent), whereas among men, these numbers were 197 and 16.1 percent, respectively (see Table 1). After carefully noting how individually they were "different" or "atypical," nearly one-third of female focus group participants proceeded to stereotype other women. The most prominent stereotype to emerge was the archetypical "mean girl," characterized as competitive, unsupportive, and eager to create drama.

According to some of the female focus group participants, women's unbridled competitive nature surfaced in multiple arenas of work ranging from physical fitness to career advancement to gaining male attention. Maddie bristled at physically competitive women, telling the group, "I'm so sick of the females that you get that come in immediately – 'I did 99 push-ups. How much did you do?'" Shifting gears, Amaya pivoted to her perception that women are excessively competitive when it comes to career advancement and seeking out male attention. After implicating all women, Amaya summed it up by saying, "I think honestly in the military women are really competitive towards each other, especially since there's such a small population."

Many female focus group participants closely linked women's competitive nature to stereotypes of women as unsupportive of each other. Women were described as "catty" and "standoffish" to each other but not to male colleagues. Comfortably casting all women in this mold, Natalie said, "Any time I interact with any other female it's kind of like a little standoffish, more so than when they interact with other guys." Adding validity to Natalie's account of female colleagues, Bella made a point of letting the group know she has always gravitated toward "guys" because unlike women, men "aren't bitchy" and "don't judge." She confessed to the group, "I have to be honest; there's some cattiness toward other females." Bella's predilection extends beyond her friendship circle to the workplace where professionally she prefers working with men. When Bella had to work with women, she described it as a "culture shock" that "just completely threw [her] off" because she "wasn't used to working with other females." Even though Bella's experience working with other women was extremely limited, she easily generalized from it, stereotyping women as unsupportive and undercutting.

According to many women, cattiness was the preferred method women used to "tear down" each other, and it manifested in their desire to generate harmful rumors about other women. Allie located the "rumor mill" squarely at the feet of her female colleagues. "I'll be honest with you; these guys aren't starting rumors about us. It's us," to which another participant added, "Yeah. Females are catty." Attempting to counter this perception, however, on 23.6 percent of occasions, female focus group participants pushed back on these stereotypes. For example, several women observed that men were just as guilty of participating in the rumor mill. In the male focus groups, on 14.3 percent of occasions, participants challenged stereotypes and acknowledged that men were just as guilty of starting rumors and enjoying the "entertainment" value of it, particularly on deployments with more "downtime" between jobs.

But a key difference existed between the men and women in terms of how the rumor mill was described and used. Women saw rumors as a means for women to undercut or be catty to each other, promote one's self over other women, and use as a mechanism for stifling competition. In stark contrast, the men described rumors as a way to isolate women, illustrate the incompatibility between genders, and most of all highlight the "drama" women bring to the workplace. Male participants tended to use a blanket stereotype of women, describing them as "bringing drama to the table." Claiming to have "zero tolerance" for drama, Patrick succinctly summed the rumor mill up as "women bring drama to the table. Women equals drama." "Drama" often referred to the rumors that would circulate about a romantic crush that ended up creating a rift between men on a team. Alluding to the fracturing of cohesion, Joshua explained the problem of gender integration: "It's the cattiness; it's the clique forming when you have a dude and chick. It's the sexuality of it. It makes a very unpleasant work environment."

2.2.4 Sexuality

As Joshua's previous comment mentions, men's perception of sexual tension was often closely related to their perception that women bring drama, which represented another key argument against integration. Many soldiers described a "natural" sexual tension that exists between men and women. Like many of his colleagues, R.J. had worked with female soldiers, and he was complimentary of their performance, describing them as "remarkably effective in helping us achieve what we were trying to achieve." But then R.J. began to walk back his assessment of their job performance, stating that it "came at a price." The price was sexual tension and discord among the team, which R.J. views as a "natural phenomenon" that he attributed to having the "attraction factor between a man and a woman, which creates an awkward environment" regardless of "how professional we want to be." An overwhelming majority of men, and to a lesser degree women, echoed R.J.'s sentiments, viewing heterosexual indiscretions as "unavoidable," "a matter of time," and an element of human nature.

Women's sexuality was predominately constructed by men as an unavoidable distraction to teams. Foregrounding his comments in men's biological imperative to pursue women, Nick makes a heteronormative case for gender exclusion: "It's human nature. Men are attracted to women. We all can agree on that." Nick concludes that sexual tension is inevitable and therefore there are no "safeguards" that can be "written into policy" to prevent it. Likewise, based on his experiential knowledge, Jimmy frames sexual tension as unavoidable and harmful to the work environment: "You get the opposite sex in close quarters and a stressful environment a long way from home and things are going to happen." Jimmy's comments underscore the disruptive influence "the attraction factor" could have on eroding professionalism between the sexes.

Men often linked their inability to control themselves around women to their self-described alpha male personalities, which they saw as biologically fixed and a prized trait that was necessary to succeed in SF. Ethan was irritated with what he perceived as conflicting professional expectations – exhibiting aggressive traits and sexual self-control: "The men you want for combat, the most driven, are also the most sexually driven men. And when you arouse one on purpose, it promotes the other as well." According to Ethan, sexual aggression goes hand in hand with being "driven," which is incompatible with having women on SF teams.

In these focus group exchanges, men talked passively about women's sexuality while actively discussing the detrimental impact it has on men. Noah reflected on his work experience with a woman, grousing that "the female that came to us was a distraction and there was, for a lack of better term, sexual frustration." Noah's comments make it clear that the problem was not the woman per se; rather, it was the uncomfortable "sexual frustration" men experienced. Although Noah identifies the men as having an adverse reaction, he is oblivious to the fact that his stereotyping of men unintentionally places blame on the "female" who was a "distraction" simply by her presence – not by her actions. Jacob sees even more dire consequences, adding that sexual tension, harassment, and even assault are "going to increase" if women are put in an environment where they are "secluded with alpha males." Jacob is referencing the potential for sexual violence perpetrated by men, and he too is oblivious to the way he is endorsing myths about sexual violence (e.g., victim blaming) by positioning integration as the true culprit.

While infrequent, a few participants challenged their colleagues' portrayal of sexuality as biologically fixed, and uncontrollable in men. Isaac pushed back on the idea that the potential for sexual tension warrants preventing women from entering SF. He argued that while some men may have a hard time containing themselves, an absence of self-control is not something that all men suffer from:

> I hate to point my finger at other SF guys, but it really falls on our shoulders that it's our fault, and I hate to say it, but why is it a big deal? Why can't you handle it, dude? The mentality around it just doesn't make sense to me. I get the problem, but it's not a problem I have.

Isaac emphasizes that he does not fall prey to this issue but also acknowledges that many of his male colleagues cannot help but experience sexual tension with female colleagues. In contrast to many of his male colleagues, he puts the onus of responsibility on men rather than holding women accountable for men's behavior.

In a different focus group, after listening to his colleagues ruminate about women's sexuality as an onsite liability, Paul countered their stories with his own extensive experience working with women:

> My experience was actually quite different than what's been voiced so far. They were absolutely an asset. I ran over 100 missions with them, over 250 with the team, and never once was I driven into their bed from sexual tension. It was just a professional relationship. We have grown men and introduce females to the equation and all of a sudden, we become animals?

Paul discusses women as subjects in this passage, pointing to their profession-alism and contributions to his missions. Taking an unpopular stand, he also unmasked the absurdity of the stereotypes being expressed by his colleagues about the inevitability of men's sexual drive and concludes that it is used as an "excuse" to oppose integration.

Matching more closely to Isaac's and Paul's opinions, female focus group participants discussed sexuality in dramatically different terms. Seeing it as neither biologically fixed nor inevitable, their conversations primarily centered on how their sexuality marked them as "different" or singled them out for unwanted attention, isolation, or harassment. Angela felt ill equipped to deal with the "dynamic" created by her presence even though she consciously downplayed her sexuality. Likewise, Jennifer and her female colleague did not "invite" male attention; nonetheless, their male colleagues reacted to their presence on the base:

> Within one month the atmosphere of that team changed due to attention. I worked with the medics in the clinic. And one of the other men on the team needed that attention from his friends and he perceived that I was getting that attention. That male/female type relationship. And we started noticing things would change. There were certain rules where we couldn't go certain places anymore on the base. And it got to the point where there was animosity in the air. And you could feel that it was towards us, for just being females and just trying to do our job.

As Jennifer notes, although she was doing nothing more than her job, the "atmosphere" changed. Some of her male colleagues struggled with the presence of two women on the base, effectively altering the dynamic for everyone. Nonetheless, Jennifer and her female colleague became culpable for the tension and experienced the consequences. Their mobility on the base was restricted, and they experienced animosity "for just being females."

Echoing the dire need for cultural reform, Charlie confided to the focus group that she was also marked for harassment because she was female. At Charlie's site, her arrival threw her male colleagues off guard because they were expecting a man to arrive: "They thought I was a dude because of my name." Her isolation and the harassment directed toward her quickly escalated:

> I guess you could say I've never experienced sexism until I got to Afghanistan, and I've never been so lonely in my life. They treated me horrible. I'm talking like a lesser human being. Like I'm sitting here eating and [they] knocked my dinner out from me, telling me, "clean that shit up bitch." Like that's how I was spoken to. [It was] just appalling.

As a petite, attractive woman of color, Charlie had been subjected to inappropriate innuendos and suggestive, racialized euphemisms in the past. However, this assignment transcended those experiences and entered a new terrain of blatant harassment. Even though her stateside superior was concerned for her and gave Charlie permission to return early, she declined. Fearing that she would not receive "good" assignments in the future and she would acquire a reputation as being too soft or too girly, Charlie suffered in silence during this deployment.

2.3 Conclusion

The overt and brazen harassment targeted at Charlie is easily identifiable, but it is also exceptional compared to the less visible obstacles to women's success that persist in the day-to-day work environment. Throughout this section, we have examined organizational resistance to change through the manifestation of organizational obliviousness, which is the hidden – and routinized – practice of relying on gender stereotypes to shape and influence beliefs and actions. Across focus groups, one of the most persistent findings was participants' normalization of gender stereotypes, particularly when opposing gender integration. As Schein (2010) has pointed out, resistance to cultural changes in an organization is a product of individuals' anxiety about the impending changes. Resistance becomes even more acute when the change, in this case gender integration, disrupts individuals' assumptions that have defined them and their place in an organization, which is what we found in the focus groups.

As we have seen, men and women held deeply embedded stereotypes about gender. Regardless of the stereotype being used, gender was constructed in binary terms that underscored men's position as belonging to the organization while defining women as outsiders, thus re-inscribing the "gendered organizational logic" structuring the institution (Acker 2006; Britton 2000). Although the majority of people were oblivious to their invocation of gender stereotypes, most of their opinions pertaining to integration and, as importantly, their daily interactions with colleagues were foregrounded in them. The few times individuals challenged stereotypes, their voices were quickly silenced by most of the focus group participants who confirmed stereotypes for one another, which simply reinforced organizational obliviousness to gender inequity. Functioning as the "invisible hand," stereotyping continues to reinforce and normalize gender hierarchies in the workplace (Ridgeway 1997).

Organizational obliviousness resides at the individual level but does not end there. When gender stereotyping is confirmed by significant numbers of organizational actors with similar beliefs, it becomes reinforced at the cultural level and helps to maintain gender hierarchies within SF and the military writ large. In turn, culture structures practices and policies that have consequences for leadership and the prospect of gender equity.

3 Entrenched Resistance at the Cultural Level

> I'm not disagreeing that in black and white women aren't allowed in SF. I'm not disagreeing there's a problem. Obviously, that's why we're sitting down. I'm saying there needs to be a culture change within the military; they need to stop making it such a big deal.
>
> (Stephanie, Participant)

In Section 2, we focused on how organizational obliviousness manifested through individual stereotypes rooted in social constructions of gender. This obliviousness becomes further embedded in the organization through the normalization of collective stereotyping that reinforces the dominant culture of the organization where it often remains invisible. As Stephanie intimates earlier, the military has a formal policy that excludes women from SF; as she stresses, a cultural hurdle remains unaddressed. However, resistance to change, particularly among organizational members who embody the existing culture, can be fraught because their culture tells them "who they are, how to behave toward each other, and how to feel good about themselves" (Schein 2010, p. 29). Changing organizational culture can produce significant anxiety among members because it erodes the assumptions they have been using to derive comfort and understanding about themselves (Schein, 1990, 2010).

In this section, we examine organizational culture and how the masculine identity of the military is re-inscribed as the dominant culture, which shapes the norms and day-to-day practices that create obstacles for gender inclusion. We explore two key arguments soldiers deployed to resist gender integration. The first argument coalesced around the language of cohesion. Soldiers frequently used cohesion arguments to sidestep discussions of fairness, equity, or individual opportunity when discussing integration; instead, they focused on how integration would disrupt the cohesive culture of the organization that they believed already worked well. The second argument centered on women's inability to thrive in the SF environment. Although men saw their actions as unique to them as individuals, they often generalized the mistakes of one woman to implicate all women as incompetent. Finally, we take a closer look at the strategies women employed to navigate the masculine culture of the military.

3.1 The Masculine Identity and Organizational Culture of the Military

Organizational culture is often described as the shared norms and values among organization members (O'Leary, 2014; Kotter & Heskett, 2011; O'Reilly & Chatman, 1996; Hatch, 1993). This broad definition of culture is helpful in providing scholars with a shared foundation. Schein (1990) provides a detailed model broken into three levels of analysis: artifacts, espoused values, and assumptions. *Artifacts* include "all the phenomena that you would see, hear, and feel when you encounter a new group with an unfamiliar culture" (Schein, 2010, p. 23). Applying this concept to the army, uniforms, saluting higher-ranked officers, and beginning or ending verbal responses with "sir" or "ma'am" would all be considered artifacts. *Espoused values* are "what people say is the reason for their behavior, what they ideally would like those reasons to be, and what are often their rationalizations for their behavior" (Schein, 1984, p. 3). While "the underlying reasons for their behavior remain concealed or unconscious" (Schein, 1984, p. 3), espoused values provide a basic understanding for how organizational members are justifying their behavior. *Assumptions* are the practices within an organization that are often difficult to discuss because they "have become so taken for granted that you find little variation within a social unit" (Schein, 2010, p. 28).

3.1.1 Masculine Identity

In the military, masculinity has specific rules that have been constructed over decades and have become the bedrock of its culture. Hegemonic masculinity, and the cultural scripts it provides, is one of the reasons many men join the military (MacKenzie, 2015; Hinojosa, 2010). Throughout our survey and focus group results, soldiers pervasively embraced a binary understanding of gender that was reinforced by the organization's masculinized culture, which demonstrated "little variation within a social unit." However, men consistently ascribed to and expressed a higher frequency of stereotyping that they often embedded in the larger context of the military's male identity. Men stereotyped themselves, priding their hyper-masculinity, which included a focus on violence, sexuality, and vulgar language in the team room. They presented a workplace culture that was grossly at odds with their stereotypical images of femininity to underscore their opposition to integration. Women also recognized and engaged with their construction as "other" in the context of the military workplace, perpetuating stereotypes of other women, while presenting themselves as exceptions who could manage the masculine culture of the organization.

SF is a space defined by the homosocial nature of a male-only workforce, where exclusivity is part of the masculine identity (MacKenzie, 2015). Male participants therefore perceived gender integration as antithetical to the espoused values of SF, even though women have been successfully integrated into other aspects of the military. Only 16 percent of male survey respondents strongly or somewhat agreed that "females should have the opportunity to serve in Special Forces" compared to 70 percent of female survey respondents. Yet, while most female respondents wanted women to have the opportunity to compete as individuals who may qualify to participate in SF, they nonetheless supported the normalized masculine identity of SF. Most survey participants reported that SF should remain masculine in nature if integrated. Roughly half of the women agreed or strongly agreed (56 percent) that SF should remain basically masculine, while most of the men agreed or strongly agreed (86 percent) with the same statement. These survey results illuminate the "taken for granted" assumptions soldiers hold about the masculine culture of SF. Referencing the hyper-masculine sports culture of professional football, focus group participants frequently analogized SF to the National Football League, with no room or need for women.

After making this comparison, Joel posed a question to the focus group: "Here's a question. They are so hell bent on doing this, on integrating women into every facet in the military, why don't they integrate women in the NFL? I mean it's the same concept. We're so hell bent on this integration of everybody. I mean it's just not necessary in this job." In a different focus group, Carter asked similar questions: "What's the difference between the professional organization like Special Forces versus the NFL? Do they have the opportunity as a female to go play football in the NFL and kick the winning field goal? So why should Special Forces?" Both Joel and Carter articulate a common perception among male focus group participants – the integration of women into SF was an unnecessary decision to symbolically "make women be seen as equals." When drawing parallels between the exclusive masculine culture of SF and the NFL, they failed to recognize the profound differences between the NFL's corporate interests and the US Army's bureaucratic mission to serve the interests of the federal government. From their lens, gender integration into SF was viewed as an intrusion into their exclusive, masculine space. They were oblivious to the ways in which their arguments reflected and reinforced the belief that women's roles should be limited by basing their qualification on one criterion (e.g., physicality), making equality an inherently impossible goal to achieve.

Under their banner definition of masculinity, many of the men in our study connected their masculine identity to the culture of SF with their personal life outside of work. They engaged in hunting, drinking, shooting, and listening to "rock-n-roll," which they defined as activities women do not enjoy. Joe highlights this in his comment about what he sees as the culture of SF and what real SF soldiers do: "Interest in the same things pretty much. We all like guns, we all like lifting weights, we all like women, we all like just being aggressive monsters on the battlefield. That's what we do." Joe made it clear that his understanding of masculinity, which he assumed was universal for all Green Berets, requires men to "like" the same activities. He assumed that women do not participate in these activities despite the reality that female soldiers operate guns, lift weights, and perform on the battlefield. By integrating these activities into his stereotype-driven definition of heterosexual masculinity, Joe articulated

a picture of an environment where women could not be included. In his understanding, masculinity requires uniformity, and SF requires masculinity.

Even when challenged with alternative views of heteronormativity, men in
our study pushed the idea that a man's ascription to a masculine identity and an
adherence to the masculine culture of SF could transcend his sexual orientation,
whereas women could not. For Jack, the Don't Ask Don't Tell Repeal Act of
2010 led him to reassess his opposition to allowing homosexuals in SF:

> I found out after the policy came through, there was a guy on my team. One
> of the most combat-driven soldiers I've ever seen. He's got everything on his
> chest, multiple awards, every school we've gone to – he was gay. He'd been
> living with a guy for years. Nobody knew about it. His off-time he would be
> hanging out with girls because he didn't want to be seen as a gay man. So, my
> whole opinion changed immediately after I saw that. I'm like, this guy's my
> best soldier. He's the best soldier in the battalion and he's gay.

According to Jack, so long as a soldier sufficiently presents himself as masculine and embraces a uniform understanding of masculinity, his sexual orientation can be overlooked.

Likewise, Zach does not see homosexuality and masculinity as incompatible:
"There is no physiological difference between a gay and straight man, but there
is between a man and a woman." Picking up with this conversational thread,
Steve succinctly stated, "at the end of the day a man is still a man." These men,
like many other male focus group participants, were oblivious to the fact that
a gay man can participate in masculinity in a way that women never can by
attributing the performance of masculinity to biology rather than culture. Their
oblivion cements the culture of the organization with the sex of its members,
regardless of sexual orientation. Thus, in the context of the masculine culture of
SF, integration does not make sense.

3.1.2 Masculine Organizational Culture

Binary gendered ideals are so infused into the masculine culture of the organization that they manifest in unexamined assumptions that lead to actions. For
example, men in our study saw women's privacy and bodily needs as distinct
from their own, which was reflected in the frequency of male focus group
discussions (126 mentions) centered on their opposition to sharing bathroom
facilities with women, which was reflected in the survey responses as well.
Thirty-three percent of male survey respondents were unwilling to use unisex
bathrooms, whereas fewer than 10 percent of women were unwilling. As
Bird (2003) argues, while men in male-dominated workplaces will often
come together to "resist women as equals" (p. 582), one of the reasons for

this could be the "comfort" ideals men construct about what it means to be with other men, even in something as basic as having an exclusive bathroom space designated for men. Bird posits that while men undoubtedly benefit from mixed-sex workgroups, they find it easier to "be themselves" when focused on specific ideals of masculinity (p. 599).

In this case, it led male soldiers to police the physical spaces of SF even though it created additional barriers for women like Judy when they were participating in trainings that have historically been closed to women. Judy "felt very happy" to have the opportunity to participate in the leadership course. She noted with pride that she "had to meet all their standards," which she felt put her on an equal playing field with her male colleagues. However, Judy faced an immediate disadvantage because she "had to wait for the males to get out of the bathroom" before she could use it. Consequently, she was always the last one to arrive to class in the morning and after breaks. Her male peers and instructor were oblivious to Judy's disadvantage; therefore, her tardiness gave them the impression that she did not take the class as seriously as her male peers, when in reality it resulted from men's preservation of the bathroom space.

Moving beyond issues of male comfort, Penner (2012) argues that bathrooms reflect the operation of power; thus, challenges to the status quo arrangements are often "bitterly contested" because they disrupt existing hierarchies. This cultural imperative is easy to discern when someone shows up to disrupt the status quo. For most men, the prospect of sharing facilities with women upsets this rhythm, which was reflected in the tight tone of Jordan's question to the focus group, "Are they going to let females just openly shower in the team room?" While Jordon pondered the idea of shared bathrooms, for other men, like Ricardo, sharing facilities did not register as an option; rather, he viewed segregated facilities as the only path forward:

> You've got to think about infrastructure development and support when you have two genders. When you're in the jungle, you have to have two separate latrines, two separate sleeping areas. It's going to cost money. You have a team room, and it has a shower. Well, now you've got to have a separate shower in the team room. It's going to cost.

Integrating women into this space, where men are neutral and women bring in gendered and embodied concerns, threatens the perceived cohesion of symbolic domination over others (Hinojosa 2010, p. 179).

These ideas pull from Cartesian models of the separation of body and mind, wherby women are the embodied ones that bring challenging circumstances, and men are disembodied and at the top of a hierarchy of value, which was captured in the rhetorical question Karl posed to the focus group, "Well are you trying to give her an opportunity or are you trying to take the risk of ruining an organization?" Answering his own question, Karl went on to say, "the juice isn't worth the squeeze. I don't see how the combat effectiveness could be raised to the point where it would offset the troubles it'll cause. We're not going to gain enough to make it worth it." Karl, like many other focus group participants, downplayed the value of equity, saying that working toward gender integration would steer SF away from its current effectiveness and potentially ruin the organization.

Male focus group discussions surrounding resources further capture this separation of the embodied challenges women's presence creates compared to the disembodied (or status quo) operation of SF. On 127 occasions, men framed integration as a waste of resources to accommodate a "handful" of women who might be interested in SF. Illustrative of this position, after listing out the military's limited resources, Clayton asked his focus group if it "is worth it at the end of the day" to pursue integration for a woman who didn't want to be a "princess when she [was] a little girl" and instead "she want[ed] to be Rambo." Clayton's remarks underscore Acker's (2006) contention that ideal-type bureaucratic organizations are inherently gendered; they have been defined, conceived, and structured with a masculine distinction and will therefore reproduce these differences and advantages in two key ways. Clayton advances masculine notions of gender that reproduce differences by constructing most women as princesses who do not belong in the masculine, cloistered space of SF, while marking the woman who doesn't adhere to his binary construction of gender as atypical. Clayton's sentiments were shared widely among male survey respondents. Seventy-eight percent believed the costs associated with integration were "sizable and probably not worth the investment" or "excessive and not worth the investment." Fewer than 24 percent of their female colleagues agreed.

Even as more women enter the military, Enloe (2000) argues that the emphasis on gender differences will continue to be used to keep women in subordinate positions and maintain hegemonic masculinity, which has also been used to exclude women from significant portions of the military. One of the traditional ways that men have resisted women's integration into military positions is through the discussion of physical standards. Cohn (2000) explored this area and argued that current white male members of the military brought up "standards discourse" as an "objective" way to argue that women have no place in the military. She argued that discourse about standards is often a way for men to resist women's integration and reject them as colleagues, in ways that appear to be gender-neutral but in practice reinforce traditional understandings of masculinity.

Resisting integration through an "objective" discourse on physical standards was common in our study as well. Physicality arguments emerged 351 times in the focus groups, but the majority (291) of those arguments originated with men compared to 54 mentions in the women's focus groups. Aside from three occasions, women framed the discussion of physicality as a difference that was being bridged with new physical training, technology and other innovations. In contrast, most discussions by men (218) centered on women's inability to physically perform the skills needed to serve in SF.

Arguing against integration, Jeremy asserted, "their bodies are not set up to do the operations we do." Bart offered additional support for Jeremy's position: "I've had supervisors that are females. Nothing wrong with them. They can work academically as a private, squad leaders or section sergeants. Just physically, [they] were unable to do some jobs." A few male focus group participants ceded that a select number of women could physically perform the job but "not the majority" of women, leading them to return to the question of the value associated with integrating "a handful" of women when the costs associated with integration were high.

Most male focus group participants, like Silas, framed their comments "objectively," often underscoring their belief that their objections were not related to gender but rather "facts." He prefaced his remarks with a disclaimer, "it has nothing to do with the female," and then proceeded to assert, "they couldn't physically do what we do." Our survey underscored this sentiment. When asked directly about integrating women into SF, 95 percent of male survey respondents said it is "very important" to keep the physical standards the same for women. Many female survey respondents (62 percent) also believed it is "very important" to have the same standards.

However, one key difference between men's and women's positions, as captured in the focus groups, is that men view the standards as a way to exclude most women. Summing it up, Jacob declared, "So long as we don't remove those measures, I honestly think there'll be very few women who will make it through." Conversely, women view gender-neutral standards as a way to potentially gain acceptance among their male peers. As Mickey notes, "if they do integrate they need the physical standards to be absolutely the same. All the standards need to be the same for that female to integrate [and] be on equal par." According to Mickey, enforcing the same physical standards will help women gain acceptance and equality with a group that culturally prides itself on its male exclusivity.

However, like most soldiers, Mickey was oblivious to the fact that women have been prohibited from the places where they could acquire many of the skills needed to compete for SF. The military has historically set standards that are institutionally unavailable for women. Being oblivious to this truism, soldiers can use standards as an easy focal point for men and, to a lesser degree, women to reinforce the cultural norm that men are the only soldiers physically capable of handling the expectations of SF, which Veronica astutely pointed out:

> The concern that I would have for the females attempting [SF] is that the qualification course tests you on a lot of tactical skills that I did not grow up with [in the army]. I have never done infantry, I've never been to Ranger school. So, I would have to learn what [men] know just to be able to survive even the selection phase. As far as the standards, I would have to train up.

Veronica recognizes that she lacks an equivalent level of preparedness for competing for a spot in SF, particularly a background in warfare tactics that many of the men she would be competing against have as part of their past infantry service. This avenue was not available for her to access because the institution barred women from combat.

Physical standards, however, exist within the larger masculine identity of the military, which means simply requiring the same physical standards will not change the organization's culture or create equity. As Schein (1984) points out, espoused values (in this case, maintaining standards) provide an ideal reason for behavior, but digging deeper, organizational values can be a veil to justify an inequitable organizational culture. The issue of cohesion is one key area where upon closer examination, the espoused value often provides cover for justifying organizational inequity.

3.2 The Coded Language of Cohesion

Team cohesion is fundamental to the functioning of SF, given its mission to carry out small-group operations in austere environments. While preserving cohesion is crucial to the successful functioning of SF, many have also used it as an argument against gender integration. Among the 90 percent of male survey respondents who opposed having women in SF, 35 percent identified the disruption of cohesion as the "single most important factor in shaping [their] opinion." When an SF team is not deployed, it spends most of its time training and planning in an ODA Team Room, where cohesion is fostered. According to focus group participants, part of the relationship building emerges from the "anything goes" environment of the team room. SF members have a tacit agreement that what is said and done within the team room "stays in the team room." This arrangement provides SF members with a safe environment where they can decompress the physical and emotional toll of the previous mission within a protected space free from the scrutiny of colleagues who are unable to relate to the unique hazards SF troops confront while deployed.

However, the team room serves another purpose. It reifies the hyper-masculine identity and culture of SF where members construct rules of engagement away from the gaze of the army's policies, regulations, and oversight. Any type of slang, profanity, racial epitaph, and the like are fair game in the team room. Trey succinctly captures the relationship between developing cohesion and the no-holds-barred team room culture: "Part of the tightness of the team of an ODA is our ability to be totally unprofessional with each other."

For many men, the culture is necessarily disrupted by the presence of women. Even if women are not advocating for cultural changes, most male focus group participants viewed their presence as a disruption to the homosocial masculinity of SF, which was also reflected by survey respondents. Sixty-seven percent of male respondents reported that if the army becomes less male dominated, it would greatly or somewhat hurt cohesiveness. Ted points to these changes in very concrete ways, noting, "So you just have to reset everybody's clock. Hey everybody, we've got a chick coming to the team room. No dick and ass jokes. Look around the team room and make sure there's nothing on the wall that's inappropriate, and just keep it professional." For Ted, women in the team room means that jokes, interactions, and décor must change. Likewise, Antonio sees women as a damper on the team's good times, "wallpapering someone's locker with tampons. It's pranks like that, that now automatically become a sexual harassment legal issue."

The impetus for the change falls squarely on gender integration. As Ted and Antonio point out, allowing women into this male enclave threatens the identity, and thus the cohesion, of SF because it will potentially change the way their teams behave and interact. Like many of their colleagues, they discuss these changes as happening when women enter the organization but do not necessarily argue that women are purposefully causing it. The survey results largely echoed their opinion. Sixty-three percent of male survey respondents overwhelmingly believed that the presence of women in SF would create tensions that would have a "mostly negative impact" on cohesion, and an additional 33 percent believed it would have a "somewhat negative impact." Moreover, 89 percent reported that placing limitations on language or behavior that "encourages soldier comradery" would "somewhat or greatly hurt unit cohesion."

Cohesion, as an espoused organizational value, serves multiple purposes. On the one hand, it fosters a team's ability to function successfully in the field and provides a much needed space for soldiers to recover from the stress of their deployments. But on the other hand, cohesion has been used as a rationalization for preserving the hyper-masculine culture and exclusively male groups in SF free from outside scrutiny. Throughout focus groups, men frequently discussed the changes they would have to make to the team room to accommodate women (e.g., clean up language or remove offensive posters). However, by virtue of making these changes, they would be acting differently around women and creating an environment where women would always be viewed as outsiders. Men's construction of cohesion is tied directly to their stereotypical performance of masculinity, which is reinforced by the culture of the institution. Their obliviousness to this dynamic restricts the ways cohesion can be imagined and structured; thus, building cohesion with women is perceived as an impossibility. In addition to seeing gender integration as inimical to unit cohesion, soldiers frequently invoked anecdotal stories about individual women to reify the masculine culture of SF and illuminate all women's incompatibility with SF.

3.3 A Woman's Missteps

Organizational obliviousness was further reinforced at the cultural level through men's tendency to draw on an anecdote about one woman and generalize it to condone all women. Male focus group participants commonly tokenized women or discussed their missteps (151 occasions), using a negative story based on one woman as a stand-in to label all women. These anecdotes often derived from hearsay and rumor or were loosely related to men's experiences working with women. Nonetheless, these stories were offered as evidence of women's professional incompetence. These uncontested stories operated as an "invisible hand" of gender bias because they were routinely confirmed by most of the focus group participants who likewise overlooked the validity of equating anecdote with evidence.

Women's professionalism was discussed in a variety of anecdotal ways during the focus groups, but the punch line was typically the same – women were incompetent. For instance, Christopher pointed to the ways that he sees women actively trying to use their femininity to get out of punishments or lighten their own workloads: "I mean probably most people that have worked with females know situations where they've spun things and it's very easy for them to play that card and not get the same punishment that men can get. So that'd be one of the challenges I could see leaders having." According to Christopher, all women would "play the gender card" to get out of punishments or change their workloads in SF, which would place additional challenges on leaders.

Marcus offered a variation of Christopher's anecdote, universalizing from his experience working with two women in the field to implicate all women:

> We had [two] females on the camp. And they were trained. They understood security; they just failed to pull security. They understand the tactics. They

just can't employ them. They get more wrapped up in the talking, and they got ten guys that are surrounding them so they feel secure. We never feel secure. That's why we always pull security.

Marcus finished his story by mentioning that this scenario "was pretty common" even though he is basing it on his interactions with two women. In Marcus's scenario, the two women were trained on security detail, but like Christopher's anecdote, they played the gender card to shirk their responsibilities, opting instead to gossip and let the men pick up their workload.

Wesley's recounting of a woman's missteps portrayed a far direr picture of a woman that he used to illustrate all women's inferior skills. Wesley prefaced his story by telling the focus group, "I've never seen any mission fail or get dropped just because there wasn't a female on the team. . . . But I have seen them go catastrophically wrong when there was a female attached." He went on to tell a story about a time he worked with a female medic who was unable to pick up a wounded soldier and carry him back to the helicopter because he was too heavy. Wesley had to "break security to pick that guy up with all his gear." On the helicopter, the female medic was working on an American soldier and a young boy from the area; a bomb injured both of them. She cried while working on the young boy because he reminded her of her son. The boy died, and the soldier survived. Although Wesley briskly mentioned, "there was too much trauma for the kid, not her fault," he proceeded to say the female medic "could have done more to help out instead of breaking down crying"; he ended his story revisiting the fact that this mission went "catastrophically wrong and almost fail[ed]" because there was a female on it.

While telling this story, Wesley criticized the medic's crying rather than describing it as a normal reaction to stress. He did not discuss the limitations of the female medic's training regarding picking heavy men off the ground, nor did he highlight her medical skills that saved the life of the soldier. Instead, Wesley labeled the whole mission as "catastrophic," emphasizing the medic's emotionality and glossing over the nature of the boy's injuries, which regardless of her crying were fatal. However, Wesley told this story about one woman to illustrate to the male focus group that including any woman on a mission creates a potential hazard.

Even though men frequently invoked universalizing anecdotes to describe women's incompetence, the survey results painted a more nuanced picture. When men were asked "how did working with female SOF [Special Operation Forces] personnel influence your ability to complete your mission" while deployed, about 18 percent reported a mostly or somewhat positive impact, 36 percent reported a "mixed impact," and 31 percent said it was a somewhat or mostly negative impact. Yet, during the focus groups, men were oblivious to the ways in which holding up a woman's missteps and generalizing them to all women reinforced the gendered culture of the organization and created invisible barriers for women.

However, women were not. In sharp contrast to the men, female focus groups discussed the inherent unfairness of holding one woman up as a token or using the missteps of one woman to represent all women (95 occasions). They pointed out the unfair, and often irrelevant ways men used unrepresentative anecdotes to question their ability to succeed in these spaces. Makayla expressed frustration over her male colleagues' references to civilian women to argue that female soldiers were ill suited to SF, "I was talking to somebody the other day and they were like, 'oh women couldn't do [SF] because all my previous girlfriends they couldn't do it.' You're like, what? What does that pool of girls have anything to do with it?"

Aside from making unfair comparisons between female civilians and female military personnel, women were also aware of the burden that their actions or missteps represented for all women. As Kristina succinctly stated, "if a male does something bad they're an exception. 'This guy just slipped through the cracks. He's a bad egg. He's a lone worker.' A female does bad and you just ruined it for everybody." Lilian pointed to a similar phenomenon when it comes to evaluating women's ability to succeed in highly competitive programs such as Ranger School:

> It's the same thing as like with Ranger School where two girls go and they both don't make it. "It's because they're females they don't have the stamina to make it," whereas like a hundred guys go and only twenty-five make it through. You're not looking at the seventy-five and going, you guys are a bunch of s--t bags. It's like, Ranger School is hard. But [men] look at those two girls.

Kristina and Lilian make it clear that women and their individual experiences become essentialized in the military and represent all women, while men are given a lot of latitude regarding their skills and talents without damaging the reputation of all men.

3.4 Proving Themselves: Strategies Women Use

The norms, traditions, and practices of the organization are made up from more than just individual behavior. Much of the masculinization of the organization has become routinized. In turn, like other male-dominated organizations (Portillo 2010), female soldiers have developed and adopted a myriad of strategies to operate within this masculine environment (Sasson-Levy, 2003;

Herbert, 2000; Kimmel, 2000). Sasson-Levy (2003) found that women took on the mannerisms of male soldiers while downplaying sexual harassment. Kimmel (2000) argued that women adopted strategies that focused on their identities as soldiers, distanced themselves from other women, and proved their ability to physically compete with men, while they maintained feminine practices in social situations.

Women in our study navigated the organizational culture in a variety of ways ranging from isolating themselves to taking additional risks to prove their competence in an environment where women were often constructed in limited, dichotomous terms. Capturing this dynamic, Shira remarked that male colleagues saw female colleagues in one of two ways: "You're a bitch or a whore. Those are your options." Evelyn echoed this sentiment noting, "You're either standoffish or a slut." Women tried to counter this traditional virgin/whore dichotomy by carefully maneuvering around these binary identities, which are rarely referenced for men in the workplace. Some women tried to behave and blend in as "one of the guys," but as Wendy explained, adopting this personality veneer doesn't work for all women: "You can't just say this is the way you should act in a male environment. For some women that might actually work kind of well, just based on her personality," but for other women "maybe not."

Other women purposefully adopted a subservient demeanor to gain acceptance without disrupting men's fragile perceptions of masculinity, but as Josefina notes, this strategy was limited to lower ranks: "If you take a role that's more subservient or working at a lower level I think that men are receptive to it. But as soon as you take on a position that is on equal footing with a male and you have that competition it's not received very well. You're labeled as a bitch." Regardless of which personality traits women cloaked themselves in, they were subjected to a constant barrage of rumors, as Tammy noted, "There's always rumors about you. If you're too nice that means you're sleeping with everybody."

Hoping to avoid similar pitfalls resulting from "just being females," other women imposed restrictions on themselves, distancing themselves to avoid rumors of impropriety. Gina described her deployment as "very lonely." She avoided her male colleagues during meals, physical training, and any downtime because she "did not want to let anybody see me in situations that could be misconstrued" as fraternization or "inviting" attention from men. Other women, like Carmen, consciously rotated their time so they would not fall victim to rumors. She described how navigating this gendered terrain could add stress to an already tense situation:

> You have to segregate yourself completely or you have to integrate yourself and be very careful. When I say a fine line, I mean it's almost nerve-wracking.

> You actually just want to be left alone because you can't just be friends like my [male] counterpart. I have no other females at all in my whole entire battalion. So, I'm just sitting here like, okay what do I do? If I go and run with this guy, then I must be sleeping with him. It's so nerve-wracking. You spend a lot of time alone.

Kate threaded the social needle carefully, choosing to be social with her male colleagues. She spent a lot of time thinking through her choices and cautiously navigating the social terrain:

> The isolation, I didn't experience that, but it came at a risk. It came at a risk of gossip and I had to be extremely cautious with it, like making sure that there were two or more [soldiers]. Even then you'd have to be like, okay there's a rumor there. I have to make sure I don't feed into this, or I've got to make sure that there's a whole squad in the room if I'm going to go hang out and play this or do that.

For other women, like Courtney, isolation was not a choice. She was ostracized from the group:

> I ate by myself for the first month. At first it was definitely lonely and hard, and I didn't know if [the battalion] would ever fully accept me. I was not only an outsider; I was not from their unit. I felt like the deck was definitely stacked against me. I was a female so that was insult to injury. I don't know if it would have been any different if I had come in as a male. I definitely still would have been an outsider, but I don't think I would have had as much to prove as a female, especially in a combat environment. I made sure that I never complained about anything, even if it sucked. I never let anything be an issue even if I felt like it probably should have been an issue. I just tried to be unflappable.

In addition to navigating social spaces, as Courtney points out, women also must prove themselves to their male peers without complaining. Among female survey respondents, 27 percent reported that they believed they needed to prove themselves to others all of time and 25 percent said most of the time. Proving one's self was not unique to women. Compared to females, male survey respondents more commonly reported that they felt the need to prove themselves all of the time (46 percent) and most of the time (21 percent). However, in the focus groups, the reasons given by men and women for needing to prove themselves were different.

Men often discussed proving themselves in terms of competing, which they viewed as a positive part of the masculine culture of SF. Proving themselves through competition helped them push one another to perform better and it fostered cohesion. Conversely, many of the women in the focus groups discussed proving themselves as a sticky hurdle to clear to gain acceptance by their male peers. As an officer, Sally explained how she felt compelled to "take the guys out [running] and make sure that I was in the top. I made sure that I beat the other male captains because I felt like it didn't matter for them, but everybody was watching me."

While Sally approached proving herself by directly competing with men, other women did not want to upset their male colleagues or be viewed as negative competition to the men currently in the organization. Rachel explained that women "need to be mindful" and rather than openly competing with men, they need to "keep it internal [and] compete with yourself and do the best that you can." She stressed to the group that "the last thing a guy wants to do is view you as competition, [and] that mentality is going to be there," which would create a chilly environment for women.

Proving themselves was not necessarily a one-time event. Many of the women in our study, like the men, changed teams or workgroups over the course of their service. As Anna points out, "You prove yourself to that team once and then you're there for however long you're with that team and you're part of the team. When you're a CST [Cultural Support Team] you're proving yourself every couple of months to whichever team you're attached to at the moment." The need to prove themselves traveled with women to each new assignment. This is particularly relevant as women consider new opportunities or promotions that would take them to new teams.

Risk taking was another strategy employed by women. It was intertwined with their need to prove that they were capable and competent in their positions, particularly as they advanced in rank, in ways that their male colleagues did not. Renee explained why she took more risks than necessary for an officer while deployed in Iraq:

> Not only was I the new person, I was the only female. There was definitely some tension in the unit. But I felt like I had to do more so they knew that I was just as serious and confident, as capable, if not more. Gunning is dangerous. It's really exhausting. So, if I wasn't leading the convoy, I was gunning. I put myself on the gunning roster. And at that time – probably still today – officers usually don't gun. I was in the turret and the battalion commander came up and he ripped the door open and he started yelling at me. He said, "what the f--k are you doing up there?" And I said, "well sir it's my turn to lead the convoy. If it's good enough for my guys, it's good enough for me." He just stopped there, and he was like, good enough answer, and shut the door.

Renee "felt like it was necessary to take bigger risks because I had to convince people that I was just as capable as the guys." Although she believed her strategy paid off with her unit, she still paid a price with her male peers, "It pissed off the male officers because they weren't going to [take these risks] so now they kind of looked bad. And that wasn't my intent. So, I kind of lost a little bit of ground with my peers but I gained the respect of my platoon."

Renee's story scratches the surface of some of the less visible cultural practices in the workplace that disadvantage women and privilege men. She tried to overcome these challenges by using several strategies including over-performing and taking extra risks in the workplace to demonstrate she was just as "serious and confident, as capable, if not more" than her male peers. But Renee's male counterparts interpreted her actions differently, intimating that she was trying to make them "look bad" even though she was trying to build rapport with the rank-and-file members of her platoon. Renee took extra risks volunteering to be the gunner on convoy missions even though male officers did not jeopardize their physical safety or compromise the subordinate-command hierarchy. Although her commanding officer reprimanded her for breaking the protocol and putting herself in danger, he was willing to overlook it because Renee explained she was gunning to "fit in" and develop a rapport with the male soldiers in her charge.

The commanding officer's acceptance of Renee's explanation highlights several aspects of working in a male-dominated organization. First, the response to Renee's breach of protocol was accepted, which validated her role as an outsider to the organization and thus her need to "prove herself" in a way that her male colleagues did not. Second, the commanding officer's actions subtly demonstrated that rules and protocol are implemented differently for men and women in the organization. To be effective as a leader, she had to work harder compared to the other male officers and subject herself to physical risks. Her superior's validation of her actions highlights the nature of organizational oblivion in the workplace. This is particularly relevant as women consider new opportunities or promotions that would take them to new teams.

3.5 Conclusion

Stereotyping is nested in and supported by the army's masculine organizational culture, which reinforces the gender hierarchies within the institution. While individuals in our study largely viewed the masculine nature of the organization as a positive, the way it manifests means that gendered stereotypes have become incorporated into the norms that permeate the institutions. Through this orga-nizational obliviousness, women are often held up to demonstrate what the culture of the military is not – meaning that individual women must prove that they belong, an invisible barrier that men in our study did not face. Moreover, male soldiers largely see potentially changing the masculine culture and male exclusivity in SF vis-à-vis integrating women as a change in the prestige of the organization. While the military is often discussed as a meritocratic institution, the homosocial nature of the organization prevents that reality, which has implications for policy change and the push to integrate women throughout the organization.

4 Entrenched Resistance at the Institutional Level

At the end of the day we are all soldiers. We take our orders from higher. So, a lot of times what's allowed to happen is what's okay with command. If there's not buy-in from the mid- to senior-ranking officers and senior enlisted, those females will not succeed. Or they will succeed in spite of their command. They will just have to be hard as hell. They will have to be willing to kind of go it alone until they prove themselves to that team. We can have things that generals say or Congress says but it really kind of boils down to that chain of command. They're going to be the ones that make sure that the guys know that they have to accept these females.

(Reginald, Participant)

As Reginald notes, policy change is enacted by Congress and pushed by the top leaders of the organization. But the policy change will only succeed if there is buy-in throughout the organization by the internal leaders tasked with implementing it, shaping the culture of the organization, and establishing the everyday practices and norms of SF. The shift in the combat exclusion policy can still be shaped by gender stereotypes. The masculine culture of the military is premised on gender stereotypes ascribed to by individuals, which in turn become scaffolded into the ways in which policies are crafted and understood at the institutional level. Inequity becomes foregrounded in this process through organizational obliviousness. Although policies are often presented as gender-neutral, an institution's members and larger culture shape how they are interpreted and implemented, which often creates inequities in the institution.

In this section, we briefly discuss gender-neutral policies and then specifically focus on three policy areas that were frequently mentioned in our focus groups and addressed in our survey: sexual harassment and violence, leave policies, and career progression. Each of these policy areas was presented as gender-neutral or explicitly focused on gender equity, but there was a lack of awareness around the ways gendered norms shaped the policies and implementation within the organization. At times, members perceived gender-neutral policies as unfairly advantaging women; at other times, they perceived policies as being fairly applied to all. Ultimately, the policy change to integrate women into combat forces in the army reveals the many ways that gender is infused in policies and norms throughout the military.

4.1 Gender-neutral Policies

Scholars have critiqued the traditional view of institutions as neutral spaces. Although organizational policies and practices may appear benign, they are often premised on faulty assumptions about gender, race, and other sociodemographic characteristics beginning with the assumed portrait of its members as white, middle-class, middle-aged men. The appearance of neutrality reinforces inequities that underlie many policies and practices, and in the case of the military create a gendered organizational logic that maintains organizational hierarchies (Acker, 2006; Britton, 2000). The obliviousness to the gendered logic of the military repeatedly surfaced in focus group discussions of policies and practices of the organization. Men discussed policies and practices on 1,567 occasions and women - on 694 occasions. Men characterized policies and practices as "objective" in 20 percent of these occasions, whereas women did so in 6 percent of them. Likewise, focus group participants couched their conversations about some policy and practices in gender-neutral language, but women were more likely to invoke it (19 percent of occasions) compared to men (7 percent of occasions).

However, the use of objective and gender-neutral language masks the underlying gendered logic of the organization, which was frequently revealed through participants' discussions of policies. During these conversations, participants explicitly made gender distinctions while referencing a policy, rule, or norm. Men discussed these in gendered terms in 72 percent of occasions and women in 75 percent. The survey results underscored the way in which soldiers see policy as gendered, beginning with "standards" applied to men and women in general. Most men (93 percent) already perceived the army standards for women as "easier" than those for men, 6 percent believed the standards were equally applied, and 1 percent believed the standards were easier for men. Women's assessments looked quite different from those of their male colleagues. Although 55 percent of female survey respondents perceived the army standards as "easier for females," more than a third (34 percent) believed they were equally applied, and 11 percent believed the standards were "easier for males." Many women, like Connie, labored under the belief that gender was irrelevant to how soldiers – and the military – viewed standards: "We all joined the military to put on the same uniform. So, we all have to have the same standard. The military did not change any standards as we got through. I have been in the military for twelve years. All those standards have been the same and it's worked."

Despite Connie's perception that the application of standards transcends gender, most people disagreed. Moreover, gendered perceptions of the existing "easier" standards, particularly among male survey respondents, colored their perspective in other areas. Among the 85 percent of men opposed to integrating SF, when asked for the "single most important factor shaping your opinion," 20 percent of them marked "other" and the most common reason listed was "lowering standards," which was a theme commonly echoed by male focus group participants. Most men assumed that the sole act of changing the policy to allow women to try out for SF would automatically result in a lessening of standards, and that women "will not be the best of the best, which is what SF is." In short, the gendered logic of the organization carried from men's assessment of the general standards being easier for women to their assumption that opening SF to women would immediately degrade the standards of "the missions, deployments, and qualification it takes to be an effective SF team member."

Women's obliviousness to the gendered logic underlying the organization manifested in their deep ascription to the ideals of meritocracy. Eighty-four percent of women supported females serving in SF. When asked for the "single most important factor shaping your opinion," the most common response (45 percent) was "the most capable soldiers should be assigned to combat, and some females are more capable than males." The second most common factor (21 percent) was "female performance in recent military operations has proven them to be an asset." In the focus groups, women often discussed their capabilities as "tools"; if they were perceived as an "asset," then acceptance by their male colleagues followed.

For Shayla, "melding with the group went seamlessly because I could physically keep up, I could do everything that they did, and I was an asset [but] I would be remiss if I didn't harp on the tension of my being there. I had nobody to talk to about it nor could I really navigate. I had no training on how to deal with the male-dominated animalistic type." Likewise, for Tonita, "[men] are assessing whether you are an asset or a liability. If the answer is that you're an asset and the answer is they didn't have to change the way that they acted, then the barriers were down at that point and the interaction was different."

Even as these women discussed their experiences of being accepted by men based on the merit of their skills, they glossed over how their experiences were impacted by the gendered logic of the organization. Shayla was unprepared for "navigating" the tension, which she attributed to the hyper-masculine environment. Tonita had to make it clear to the men that her presence would not require them "to change the way that they acted." Both women – and the men they worked with – put the burden of acceptance on women. While women understood they had to prove their skills and establish themselves as "assets," they were oblivious to the second burden they had to overcome, requiring them to adapt their behavior to gain acceptance.

A few women, however, were aware of the limitations the military, as a gendered organization, placed on their options. Isabelle, a soon-to-be major in the army, always wanted to try out for SF. As integration loomed on the horizon as a possibility, Isabelle talked about her excitement, "I would totally [try out for SF]. I pin major on in December and I was toying with the notion. Should I not pin major because if this does open up I would be outside the window to attempt to try out?" But then she started to lay bare the organizational obstacles that were in her way: "We tell ourselves as this premier force that there are no boundaries in our military, that your merit alone will set the limit on what you can do. In reality, that's bulls–t. There are positions females can't apply to." After a moment reflecting, Isabelle revealed the entrenched ways in which the gendered logic of the organization maintains hierarchies while presenting a picture of equality: "It's interesting. We have vignette briefs. There are a bunch of males and I am always selected to give the brief. Why? Because I give the appearance that we're this integrated force and you've got this female captain who can speak a tactical operation at a top-secret level. But I'm just a little mouthpiece."

Isabelle's understanding of the organization as a gendered institution represents a minority perspective. For instance, many male focus group participants voiced their support for some aspects of gender equity, while also making contradictory arguments for either excluding women or creating gender-segregated teams. Orrin states that women "certainly have a place at the table, just not on an ODA." He wants to see women remain in support roles. Thad offered a similar idea, "females have a role in Special Forces and I fully support their integration. I do not support them on ODA." He followed up his comment with a suggestion of creating "separate SF groups" for females – an idea that was floated by many male focus group participants. Thus, the entrenched and hidden way gender operates in the military surfaced in the way men characterized themselves as open minded and equitable while also maintaining current gender hierarchies.

On the surface, institutional policies and practices appear to be gender-neutral; however, the focus groups revealed that participants frequently perceive and interpret them in gendered terms. They were typically oblivious to the way the gendered culture of the institution is infused into the institutional interpretations of "equitable" outcomes. Moreover, this gendered logic flowed to the interpretations and implementation of policies related to sexual assault and violence, leave policies, and career progression and leadership roles.

4.1.1 Sexual Harassment and Violence

Paralleling the civilian workforce, covered under Title VII, Army Regulation (AR) 600–20: Prevention of Sexual Harassment (POSH) defines two types of sexual harassment: quid pro quo and hostile environment. The former is defined as "conditions placed on a person's career or terms of employment in return for favors." The latter is defined as "a hostile environment occurs [in which] soldiers or civilians are subjected to offensive, unwanted and unsolicited comments or behaviors of a sexual nature" (p. 68). To implement POSH, the army created the Sexual Harassment and Assault Response and Prevention (SHARP) program. This program "provides unity of effort for sexual harassment and sexual assault prevention efforts across the Army" (SHARP Guidebook).

Two 2004 reports indicated that many of the army's policies and procedures related to the abatement of discriminatory behavior were not widely known (*Task Force Report on Sexual Assault Policies* and *Task Force Report on Care for Victims of Sexual Assault*). In part, SHARP was developed as a response to this and was meant to push for cultural change. The military's efforts to curtail sexual assault have shown some bright spots of improvement. For instance, in 2006 a mere one in fourteen military members reported sexual assault; by 2017 these numbers improved to one in three. Another promising sign is the overall prevalence in sexual assault, which was reported to be at its lowest level in 2017 since the Department of Defense (DoD) began tracking prevalence in 2006 (Department of Defense, 2017).

However, despite these encouraging indicators, our data shows that organizational obliviousness to the gendered stereotypes underlying SHARP has led it to reinforce many of the cultural norms of discrimination it is pushing to change. A similar dynamic has been found in other research. Workplace sexual harassment training frequently stimulates and reifies, rather than disrupts, gender stereotypes, which has a polarizing impact on men and women (Tinkler et al., 2007, 2008, 2012).

Likewise, SHARP reinforces the idea that sexual harassment and assault are gendered rather than abuses of power. These gendered interpretations of sexual violence also manifest in how survivors of sexual violence interpret their own victimization. For example, male victims of sexual assault are far more likely than women to frame the assault as "hazing, bullying, physical abuse," as opposed to an abuse of power (SHARP, 2018). Although the military has stepped up efforts to address male victimization using the DoD's 2016 *Plan to Prevent and Respond to the Sexual Assault of Military Men*, our research indicates that soldiers often negatively receive SHARP and confusion exists regarding what constitutes sexual harassment.

Echoing the findings of Tinkler et al. (2008), the men in our focus groups often expressed confusion and frustration about sexual harassment policies, which amplified their fear that women will use them to disrupt the norms that structure their homosocial work environment. Preston voiced his frustration about potentially having to police his language, "Like you can't curse to a female. If you do she can file a complaint against you and then you get in trouble, then you get investigated." Similarly, according to Alan, the normal mode of operation with his colleagues will have to change, "I have to treat you differently because I'm worried for my own career as to whether or not I'm going to get a sexual harassment lawsuit." Alan's concerns were frequently expressed in focus groups. Men often lamented about the unfair interruption sexual harassment and assault allegations posed to their careers. According to the DoD's 2017 *Annual Report on Sexual Assault in the Military,* these concerns continue to reverberate among service members. Finally, discussions of SHARP highlight some of the other ways that women entering the all-male work environment may be disruptive to current workplace norms.

Given the overwhelming number of men in the military, historically the majority of sexual harassment and sexual assault victims have been male. However, women experience sexual assault at much higher rates proportional to their overall population in the military, and they report incidents of sexual assault at a much higher rate (nearly two and a half times) compared to men (SHARP, 2018). Respondents in our study pointed to SHARP as reinforcing the idea that men are perpetrators of assault and harassment while women are victims. Focus group participants specifically discussed SHARP on 114 occasions; in 62 percent of those discussion, participants characterized SHARP as being "harmful." Kim's and Cassandra's discussion of a SHARP training video in one of the focus groups is illustrative of how many soldiers discussed SHARP. Kim starts by sharing her experience:

> I was in a room with all these men – I might have been the only female in there – and we had to watch this video for training. I thought the video was incredibly biased. It was saying "oh a woman is raped every two seconds" or whatever in the military. And it was like, where are all these women? Not that it doesn't happen. But by the end of it I felt like every guy in the room was staring; well one in four women is raped and she's the only one in here. ... I felt like at the end I had to stand up and say I wasn't raped; it wasn't me.

Cassandra responded to Kim's story saying, "No, that video is ridiculous. All the women were incredibly weak or some stereotype that was carried too far. I'm very offended because I'm not like that. I've never acted like that. It was more uncomfortable than if I'd been in a room being catcalled. I could have handled that a lot more." Their exchange highlights the unfortunate way that a training meant to push for equity in the workplace in fact reinforces gender stereotypes and makes women feel their professionalism is undercut by the program's overly dramatic portrayal of all women as victims. Cassandra's and

Kim's confusion was shared among survey respondents; 26 percent reported that "the training has been confusing." Female focus groups expressed frustration over the essentialized construction of women as victims. While unintentional, the training positions women as a dependent group ironically in need of male protection from male aggression.

Women were further concerned that the army's approach to policy implementation would influence how men engage with them. As Nadia notes, "now they're literally scared for their careers to work with a woman because it's going to be some sort of sexual harassment complaint, no matter what I say." This fear does not seem to be unfounded. Many of the men in our survey (36 percent) reported that sexual harassment training "has made me afraid to interact with females in the military." This theme was just as prevalent in our focus groups when men discussed the army's approach to sexual harassment and sexual assault as instilling fear in them. Men's fear of working with women surfaced 351 times during the focus groups. Steven views the army's approach as one that favors women, making him scared to work with female colleagues: "She can take anything and go report it up as either whatever, sexual harassment, just regular harassment, equal opportunity. It will – no matter what – go bad for me." Javon similarly notes, "Sexual harassment – in the military I mean you're guilty until you're proven innocent."

Steven's and Javon's fears of working with women and their portrayal of men as the real "victims" in sexual harassment do not match the reality of sexual harassment victimization. In a 2018 nationally representative sample of adults, 81 percent of women compared to 43 percent of men reported being sexually harassed. Moreover, 71 percent of women reported experiencing verbal sexual harassment, 51 percent unwelcome sexual touching, and 34 percent being physically followed. The corresponding numbers for men were 34 percent, 17 percent, and 12 percent, respectively (Chatterjee 2018). However, male focus group participants commonly (161 occasions) discussed themselves as victims who were vulnerable to women's false accusations. Lindsey explained how the deck was stacked against all men: "Let's say a female soldier makes a complaint, sexual harassment wise, and it's totally false. The chain of command is going to support her accusation to the utmost degree."

Women, however, were far less likely to discuss men's victimization over false accusations. They only mentioned it five times, and on four of those occasions, women were disputing the validity of men's claims. A far more salient, but related, concern for women was their fear of garnering a poor reputation, being ostracized or retaliated against if they complained about harassment, which continues to underlie their trepidation in reporting (Department of Defense, 2017).

Men's exaggerated fear of being falsely accused of harassment has spillover effects that manifested in other areas such as professional mentoring relationships with women. Several men who said they supported gender integration also noted that they mentor women. But they only provide mentees with feedback with another "witness" in the room to guard against potential unfounded claims of harassment. These men explained that similar precautions are largely unnecessary when they counseled men. However, the solution to stave off future, meritless accusations was often impractical, which led mentors to provide women with critical feedback in a public forum when a "witness" was not available, whereas men received it in private. Thus, the more visible critique of women compared to men inadvertently reinforced stereotypes about women's inferior competence compared to their male peers.

Many of the men in our study confirmed the idea that they treat women differently. As Charles says, "I have to treat you differently because I'm worried for my own career." Often these were well-intentioned men who ended up treating men and women differently and reinforcing gender stereotypes. Like the male focus group participants, 29 percent of male survey respondents reported they were not at all comfortable working with women, and an additional 32 percent reported being only "somewhat comfortable."

Women were very aware of the fact that their sex stunted their interactions with male colleagues. They pointed out that men were often afraid to engage with them, since there was a culture of mistrust built on fears around sexual harassment claims. Stacey described her experience working with an all-male group:

> It's almost like a reaction from a scared dog, not looking you in the eye. It comes from – they have been preached to – and they will tell you this. They expect women to be hard to work with. Then they're like, oh wow you're a lot easier to work with than I thought. I thought I was going to end up having my career ended [because of a sexual harassment claim] if I talked to you.

Stacey's perception of how men view working with women is not unfounded. Male focus group participants discussed the filing of unfounded sexual harassment claims as widespread. In almost every focus group, someone relayed a secondhand story about a man who had a false claim made against him that ended his career, although men could rarely point to actual people who had experienced false claims, and there is no evidence supporting their claims of widespread false sexual harassment accusations being made by women in the military.

Men's discomfort with working with women leached into their fear of attracting additional scrutiny to their informal standard operating procedures if women were on SF teams. Men noted that if women were on their teams, they would have to change their practices when it came to how they treated everyone on their teams. Fearing that women could unfairly allege that they were kicked off a team because of their sex, team members explained that they would have to implement a new protocol and begin providing formal reasons for removing people (even men) from a team instead of using their current informal practice of citing a member's poor fit with the team as legitimate grounds. Kevin describes how integrating women would be disruptive:

> A few weeks go by, and it's clear the new guy is not working out. We put his stuff in the hallway, and tell the sergeant major this guy is no longer on our team. The first female shows up at her team, and let's just say, by chance, that she is that person. We do this to guys all the time. When it's done to that female, how is that going to be perceived by the outside world? It would easily be perceived as discrimination vis-à-vis just the way we do business, which is what it is. And maybe it is unfair; maybe it's not. But when you introduce that new variable you're introducing that question.

Kevin bemoans the changes that would potentially happen because women are entering the organization. He believes that if women are on a team, and if they perceive decisions as discriminatory, the team will be held accountable for its informal evaluation of team members. In a homosocial organization, where men can define and apply the rules, they do not have to provide reasons for their behavior or judgments of others. But in a mixed-gendered organization, they believe this process will be upended and they will have to document their decision making to ensure it is not discriminatory. From the male vantage point, gender integration poses an unwelcome intrusion into their daily operations. Even more troubling for many male focus group and survey participants, this new scrutiny would open them up to additional oversight from outsiders that would erode cohesion. Seventy-eight percent of men reported that having "nonmilitary people getting too involved in army affairs" would "greatly hurt cohesion," and 18 percent believed it would "somewhat hurt cohesion."

Men believed integration would infringe on other aspects of their norms and rules. Mathew described how the informal onboarding of a new member would be impacted because of women: "You get a new guy on a team there's just – I'm not going to call it initiation but you're going to push his buttons. And now if I've got a new girl on the team there's a lot of things that you're not able to do legally." New team members are subjected to a lot of "ribbing" from the seasoned members of the team, which men viewed as an aspect of building cohesion. For many of the focus group participants, like Mathew, discussions of sexual harassment and sexual violence were typically divorced from the acts themselves. Rather, men were frustrated with the oversight that comes with combating sexual harassment and sexual violence, which they believed would change their normal work practices. Even though some of these work practices may have been problematic on their own (firing men without reason or excessive "initiation" behaviors), the presence of women and the focus on sexual harassment and sexual assault were identified as the problem.

Joel directly addressed this, referring to the "gender card" that women have because of the army's focus on sexual harassment. He argued that this card is so disruptive, it is best to exclude women:

> I've had it happen a couple of times. There is this [attitude of] "I'm not getting my way. It's because I'm female. I'm not getting my way or you're basically calling my bluff on something. That's sexual harassment." Or, there is a card that can come out of the deck that is played in those situations where I'm not saying you're an idiot because you're a female. I'm saying you're an idiot because you're an idiot, period. There is an entire deck of cards there with sexual harassment and everything else that needs to be completely removed in order for us to function.

Joel, like other men in our study, argued that women could claim sexual harassment or sex discrimination if they did not get their way or if they were not provided with a reason for particular workplace behaviors. For Joel, instead of addressing this by adjusting leadership or management practices, the easiest solution is to exclude women. Roger also believes sexual harassment claims included an expansive array of actions that would require men to change their behavior while unnecessarily adding stress to the workplace: "Women in Special Forces would add another level of stress, drama, and a constant stressor that at any moment you could lose your job because of a weird look, sexist comment, or harsh joke. We are always watching our backs overseas; we shouldn't back home." Roger equates the threat of enemy combatants to that of women lying in wait in the team room to make sexual harassment allegations. He was oblivious to how his unsubstantiated claim narrowly defined who is seen as a "real" soldier within the workplace. Like other men, he lamented that they may have to adjust their behavior, even when it has very little to do with sex because they might be called upon to explain and change that behavior.

The focus on sexual harassment and sexual violence may increase scrutiny over gendered behavior that has been normalized within the organization. Rather than viewing some of the practices of the organization as faulty, men tend to locate the source of the problem with gender integration, which created obstacles for women who felt an additional burden for proving they belonged in the masculine organization. Women commonly noted that their precarious position was underscored by men's view of them as women first, and not as coworkers. As Melanie described, "when they looked at me, they saw a woman. They didn't see a soldier." Similarly, Ellen noted that changing this dynamic would require men "to realize that when you put on that uniform, and you go to war, you're US Army. You're not the female that is underneath it."

Yet, the masculine culture of the military shapes the ways in which daily practices are understood and implemented at the institutional level, which continues to quietly reify inequities at the individual level. The way the army has responded to an increased focus on sexual harassment and assault has also been met with resistance by men and women in the organization. Rather than educating soldiers that sexual harassment and assault are abuses of power used against people of all genders in organizations, SHARP reinforces the idea of male predators and female victims. At the same time, the training has fueled an exaggerated (and unfounded) fear among men that women frequently manipulate harassment claims for their own gain. These stereotypes enable men to more easily dismiss the scope and severity of sexual harassment, while providing justification for them to voice hostilities toward women who file complaints (Tinkler, 2012). The result is that men's understanding of women in the workforce remains narrowly constructed and inhibits all soldiers' ability to engage with one another professionally.

4.1.2 Leave/Non-deployment Policies

Like discussions of sexual harassment and assault, leave and non-deployment policies were often discussed in gendered ways, although these policies affect all people. In the focus groups, men and women discussed policies as gendered 1,128 and 520 times, respectively, where they underscored the different standards, rules, or norms for women compared to men. Temporary medical leave policies exemplify how policies become gendered within an organization. These policies dictate when someone can deploy on a mission, how they train with their colleagues, and when they must be reassigned or relieved from duty because of medical injury or temporary medical situations.

SF is a physically demanding career that takes a toll on men's bodies. In the military, being non-deployable because of a temporary medical issue can have devastating effects on their team, particularly in the small, twelve-person teams that deploy as part of SF. Throughout the focus groups, participants regularly informed us that twelve-man teams were rarely fully staffed because men were out due to temporary injuries. However, medical leave policies were rarely discussed in the context of SF soldiers. Rather, men centered their discussion on how women's temporary medical leave status because of pregnancy would disrupt teams and pointed to this policy as a reason to oppose integration.

As team leader Roy stressed, bringing women on to the team means he is likely going to suffer from chronic understaffing: "As a team sergeant, I have a twelve-man detachment. If I have one female who ends up pregnant for one year that means I'm losing almost 10 percent of my capability, and I'm not going to get [it] backfilled. . . . So unless they created some sort of pregnancy battalion." Here Roy jokes that there needs to be a separate unit for women because they can get pregnant and that will disrupt his ability to stay fully staffed. Although he presents the idea in jest, it was one that was embraced by many men to solve the problems associated with gender integration – including the potential for pregnancy – in an "equitable" manner. Les argued that pregnancy reinforces the perceived staffing challenges: "The army's not going to give me another person because someone got pregnant. Let's say we get to a point where a quarter ratio of our company is female, and a quarter of that quarter becomes pregnant all in the same window or within months of each other. That's going to be pretty challenging to try and fill critical positions." Both Roy and Les are resistant to gender integration because they foresee difficulty trying to staff their teams in the event of pregnancy. They are oblivious to how they deploy the leave policy as a problem with respect to women's pregnancy but overlook how the same policy creates problems for staffing all-male teams when a soldier is on leave. Neither Roy nor Les critiques the policies in the military that may prevent SF teams from temporarily back-filling positions when men are on leave. Nor do they see similarities between men's temporary medical leave and women's temporary medical leave, characterizing the former as part of the reality of being an SF soldier and the latter as a unique hardship that women would present for a team.

Women, however, pointed out that leave and non-deployment policies cover more than pregnancies. They are mainly used for injury or other medical issues. Even though these are rarely discussed the same way since medical leave is already normalized in the organization, Marianna saw pregnancy and injury in a similar light. She speculated that if women were on SF teams, the number of pregnancy leaves and medical leaves would likely be similar in the long run:

> Charlie is accidentally going to break his leg on a HALO jump right before a combat mission. What are you going to do? I'm not a mathematician or anything, but if you would take all the data from the planet earth, I guarantee the percentages almost work out perfectly, once females are in SF and they get pregnant. Two hundred years from now, I guarantee if you took all the data from a soldier breaking himself and females getting pregnant and missing deployments – it will work out.

Other women spoke about pregnancy and medical leave as a similar issue that could be managed on the team. Comparing the two types of leave, Ella explained:

> You deal with it the same way you deal with a man who has a nine-month profile. And do they have men who have nine-month profiles? Absolutely, because they break their knees, hips, joints, whatever. [Pregnancy] is a medical profile that says that they can't do certain things. It doesn't say that they can't come to work, they can't work and do their jobs. It doesn't say that they can't even be physical for a good portion of their pregnancies.

Ella points out that not only can a pregnancy leave be managed like a medical leave; she also stresses that it does not mean a person is completely absent from work. Although a significant portion of SF revolves around physical training for deployments, Ella reveals the gendered logic of the organization by reminding the group that despite the focus on physicality, several other facets of SF training are not moored to physicality.

In addition to arguing that pregnancy and medical leave can be managed the same way, women highlighted one key difference between the two that they believed undermined men's preoccupation with using the possibility of pregnancy as a reason to oppose integration – family planning. All the female focus groups raised the fact that women already plan pregnancy in accordance with their career goals. Elizabeth explained that she worked and trained for years to earn a coveted spot on a highly skilled team. Although she got married during this time and wanted to have children eventually, she planned her pregnancy around her career goals, "My husband and I waited three years to have children [because] I wanted to get done with my team time. So, I think that's what you're going to find in [the] Special Forces community as well. Women will work towards [their goal] and they'll put things off until it's a good time." Mirroring Elizabeth's sentiments, women frequently pointed out that it would be highly unlikely that a woman would opt to become pregnant once she placed on a SF team given the years of training and sacrifice she would have undergone to earn her position.

However, men were oblivious to the pragmatic ways that pregnancy could be managed or that women would (and already do) time their pregnancies around their career goals. Instead of evaluating the similarities between pregnancy and medical leave, several male focus group conversations regarding leave and non-deployment policies often devolved in a similar way as sexual harassment policies did. Namely, some men suggested that women would manipulate their pregnancies to get out of deployments or to leave the military altogether. Making an unsubstantiated generalization, Ross asserted, "females are trying to get out of deployments with pregnancy or some type of inappropriate relationship on a weekly basis in the military. Why inject that into Special Forces?" Although Ross has no data to support his generalized claim, it resonated with many men like Tanner. He "would like to think that the female who does say yes [to SF] would be unique" and put her team first. But he was concerned that she would use the "military tools" available to her, which he viewed as unfair. Tanner concluded, "the military absolutely caters to the females." Similarly, Nolan argued that women receive unfair advantages such as having the option to leave the military when they are pregnant, while men only receive limited time off to meet their child: "Female soldier gets pregnant they have an option just to exit the military. . . . If my wife has a kid I get like ten days or something like that." Instead of critiquing the institutional family leave policy for men, Nolan frames it as another benefit women receive that men do not. He is oblivious to the gender logic underlying the family leave policy and instead attributes blame to women rather than the institution.

Ross and Nolan were not alone in being oblivious to how the family leave policy and their understanding of related issues of parenting is gendered in the organization. Other men presented motherhood, but not fatherhood, as incompatible with professional obligations. Outlining the problems motherhood would present, Silvio explained, "we cannot stop her from having children – now she's pregnant. For us as an ODA, hey we'll give you time off, see the birth of your child, pack your stuff up, you're downrange. For females it's more of a closer attachment to that child. Is that going to be a distractor downrange?" According to Silvio, as a team leader he cannot dictate when women can or cannot have children, which injects some unpredictability in planning while deployed. And second, even if he accommodates a woman during her pregnancy, he cannot rely on her in the field because she will be too focused on her child. Drawing on a stereotype about women's maternal instinct, Silvio does not even consider that fathers also become attached to their children and may be "distracted downrange."

Like sexual harassment and sexual assault policies and trainings, leave and non-deployment policies shape the experience of everyone in the organization. However, they are read and discussed as primarily gendered and as a hindrance to women's full participation as employees.

4.1.3 Career Progression and Leadership Roles

Discussions of gender equity in public organizations often tie back to discussions of leadership (Sabharwal, 2015; Connell, 2006; Dolan, 2004). Public organizations have an additional layer as leadership refers to internal organizational managers and external political leaders, which was reflected in the focus groups and surveys. Soldiers discussed the institutional expectations and norms for leaders, their ability to set the tone for policy implementation regarding gender integration, and external political leaders. Overall, male focus group participants discussed leadership 719 times and women 135 times.

As male soldiers discussed leaders during the focus groups, they made it clear that male leadership is the institutional norm. Men in our study repeatedly and exclusively talked about the difficulty male leaders have successfully managing female soldiers, which they anticipated would be even more challenging in SF. Many women, however, pointed to the problematic institutional expectations and norms around leadership that they have a hard time living up to within the organization. To begin with, not only are women viewed as more difficult to manage, the survey results demonstrated that very few male soldiers are comfortable working under a female leader. Most men (74 percent) preferred working for a male boss and 25 percent had no gender preference, whereas for women, 34 percent preferred a male boss but most women (64 percent) had no gender preference.

Men's preference for male bosses was often revealed by their disparate reactions to female leaders' directives. Janelle explained how this dynamic manifested among one of her male subordinates:

> I had a soldier, he just constantly got in trouble, and my NCOs would berate him, curse at him, yell at him. I'd just go in and I'd talk to him very calmly, "hey man you're f--king up. You need to fix this." [He] said "oh you're mean. You're this and you're that." And I had to point it out to him. I said "you know, your team sergeant cursed you out for over an hour and degraded you for over an hour and I am merely telling you that you need to stop what you're doing. How is that any different?" And I said, "are you considering that maybe it's because I'm a female?"

Having few role models to turn to, some female leaders opted to modify their behavior to try to counter the difficulties they experienced from male subordinates, which they discussed during the focus groups on 290 occasions. Marcy explained, "there are certain things, the way that I talk, the way that I present myself, the way that I interact with a man that has to be modified. I'm learning every day the best way to do that. And there's not a lot of women in the military [and] there's not a lot of role models."

In addition to facing gendered treatment from subordinates, women were saddled with overcoming the expectation that military leaders were family men who understood the sacrifices soldiers make while deployed. Many women pointed to this expectation as a catch-22 for their advancement into leadership positions. Sally explained this gendered conundrum:

> If you choose to not have a family and then you get into those higher ranks, you're expected to have a family. This magical family that you made while you were climbing that ladder. You're not going to be in that position and not have a family because then you don't understand everybody that works for you. But you can't stop to have a family if you're going to make it up that high. It's catch-22.

Similarly, female focus group participants discussed the difficulty of balancing work and family life and having to make decisions between family and career on 82 occasions, which they felt unduly burdened them compared to their male colleagues. Gretchen noted that it is difficult to have a family and continue to rise through the ranks: "That's why you don't see a lot of women in the upper ranks because they choose family which is perfectly acceptable, an excellent choice, but unfortunately the army does not allow for you to be a mother and have a career." April notes that this is not unique to the military: "Once we're ready to have a family now it's choosing between having a family and having a career, and even in the civilian world the structure isn't set up to accommodate that, to accommodate being a woman in a professional field and being a mother." Similar to other professions, motherhood was seen at odds with climbing into leadership positions, even though ironically both men and women noted that there is an expectation that military leaders have families to seem relatable to most of their subordinates.

Serving in combat arms is another gendered expectation the institution has for people pursuing a high-ranking leadership position. But as Julia succinctly states, "We talk about equality and we have EO [Equal Opportunity] and yet we are excluded from certain branches," which forecloses the possibility for advancement for women who "want the opportunity." Estelle went into more detail about how this expectation has consequences for women's advancement:

> With the way the army's configured now, especially for officers, if you were not in a combat arms branch you will not get those battalion command jobs or those higher-up positions. That's why you don't see a lot of females that are generals or full birds because you don't have that combat arms experience. If you're SF or you're infantry or you had that combat arms you are looked at more favorably when it comes to promotion and when it comes to commands. But not when you're in a support element or not in a combat arms. So yes, I would think that being in SF would open doors for women. Because as it is, I think there's a glass ceiling.

Although most men were oblivious to the impossibility of women achieving this institutional expectation, some men like Zachary understood this limitation. Zachary credits his wife with opening his eyes to the inherent limitation this barrier posed for women leaders.

> I think that the women who are senior in rank resent the fact that they would've risen faster and been more respected had they been Ranger qualified because, again, the pecking order. This is an organization about killing the enemy and doing the most dangerous job. So, the infantry officer and the Special Forces officer at the table, it doesn't matter the rank. That's the person everybody turns to. And so, the women, as my wife would say, don't have a seat at that table because they're not combat arms. So, I think that really the impetus [for integration] is senior ranking officers, women, general officers, colonels that are still second-class citizens because they're not combat arms.

Combat exclusion policies along with other gendered expectations presented a glass ceiling for women desiring career advancement. Female focus groups lamented these obstacles to their career progression on 171 occasions. Several of these gendered nuances were also reflected in the results of three survey questions where men and women were asked to compare their professional development and career opportunities. In terms of mentoring, 35 percent of women reported having a formal mentor and 78 percent an informal mentor. Men's numbers were higher; 42 percent have a formal mentor and 83 percent an informal mentor. Men also more commonly participated in military professional development (52 percent) compared to 40 percent of women.

These gender differences tracked with several measures capturing soldiers' evaluation of their career opportunities compared to those of the opposite sex. While 41 percent of men reported having a completely equivalent opportunity for advancement, only 33 percent of women felt the same. Likewise, men more commonly believed women had the same training opportunities (39 percent) and assignment options (37 percent). But for women, only 20 percent believed they had the same training opportunities and a paltry 13 percent believed they had the same assignment options compared to men.

Some soldiers appealed to the norms of professionalism to overcome resistance to female leadership and integration. As Johanna notes, "We're professionals. Let's all work to the betterment of the organization." For Johanna, part of professionalism is placing the organization above individual beliefs. She acknowledges that individually men may not want to work with women but given that this is the direction the organization is heading, they should all work toward it. Similarly, Anthony points to the rules and norms of the organization saying, "The army has rules and regulations and standards. And when [women] were willing to follow standards I didn't have issues. If you treat them like soldiers with rank structure, next thing you know I don't have to worry about shower issues." While men resisting gender equity often pointed to rules or political authority over the organization as negative, men and women who

championed gender equity would regularly point to expectations of professionalism and the recognition of the policies and leadership structure.

Despite the gendered limitations of the institution, focus group members
commonly turned their conversations to discuss the important role leaders have
in setting the tone and implementing policies. Although leaders are often held
accountable for other policy failures, according to many soldiers, they get a pass
on issues related to gender equity. Kristina faults weak leaders for letting gender
inequity fester in the workplace. She was frustrated that leaders typically
focused on individual women or women as a group to solve the problem of
gender inequity when this is really an organizational issue: "The problem is not
the female's. The problem is the perception of the males that work around her.
That's not her job to fix. That issue is on the leadership to fix." Kristina is not
alone in her call for leaders to shape the organization. Raul notes, "it's our job as
leaders to provide an environment which is safe."

But some pointed to the culture of advancement for leaders in the military as
obfuscating this norm. Taylor said that to get promoted, leaders were expected
to have no complaints lodged within their units. He says, "the battalion com-
mander needs zero SHARP complaints in my company – none. And, if he
doesn't have that, he won't make colonel." He goes on to say this follows up the
chain of command. To move up in rank, individual leaders want to hold out their
units as an exemplar unit free of harassment and assault, so they may turn
a blind eye to these behaviors rather than engaging them as organizational-level
issues.

Inaction by leadership was not the only point of contention. Tom discussed
leaderships' propensity to overreact and unwittingly shift organizational norms
because of women's presence. This led the rank-and-file male soldiers to blame
women or at the very least express frustration in the way their presence changed
the norms of the workplace:

> A lot of the stuff that affected morale wasn't on [women]. It was on us. We
> had an open-air gym – instead of lifting weights with your shirt off, because
> it's 140 degrees, [the commanding officer said] "Hey guys, a female's here,
> everybody needs to have a shirt on at all times." And of course, everybody
> gets angry. The [women] were like, "Hey, it's not us. We don't care. We don't
> mind at all if you're not wearing your shirt." But leadership is so worried that
> we became very limited in having to remain covered, and dress codes, and
> everything else.

As Tom notes, the women were not pushing for changes to norms, but leadership insisted that their presence meant men had to change their norms in the
work environment. Ultimately, male soldiers primarily blamed women for this
shift in culture, even when they recognized that male leaders instigated the

change in policy and norms. Tracking with these sentiments, 63 percent of male survey respondents reported that the "tension created when females enter a new workplace [would] greatly hurt unit cohesiveness," but notably, only 14 percent of women perceived it the same way.

In addition to blaming the presence of women for institutional changes, there was also a sense among male focus group participants that the push for gender integration was coming from political leaders outside of the organization, which they gave voice to on 735 occasions. Political leaders were seen as problematically interfering with the norms of the organization, which men resisted for two main reasons. First, they believed political leaders were disconnected from the day-to-day work of the organization. Second, since it seemed to be externally imposed, many men felt as though the leaders within the organization did not want integration, so it was reasonable to resist gender equity. Capturing this reasoning, Marco stated, "women serving as SF soldiers is a joke. There is not a single operational reason to have women serving in this capacity. The whole basis of the subject screams politics and not operational readiness and capability. Stop wasting our time."

Many men also saw gender integration as "political correctness" related to society's changing attitudes toward women that were unrelated to the work of the military. Elected officials and political appointees in the DoD were described as out of touch and willing to unnecessarily shift the norms and culture of the military. Politicians and the political process were frequently presented as separate from the work of the organization. Ray says, "it just starts playing into politics; we need to have women in everything. They don't look at the end result of what could happen." Stanley noted, "the political process between here and the top – they say they know what's best for us, but if you can't ask the junior guys you're not going to know the true results."

According to Cory, integration is a "feel-good" imposition from external leaders who will change the organization negatively with little harm to themselves: "It's great in theory and it sounds good on a five-minute clip on TV. But we're the ones that have to suffer. Not somebody sitting in Washington, DC." Concurring, Luther stressed that the interference from Congress means that "those invisible standards of how team business is conducted will have to change. Every general in the chain, everybody can say this is not going to change; these are the standards. It doesn't matter, if zero women make it through, as soon as you allow that, then Congress gets involved and says well that's not fair."

John sees the fallout of integration resulting in a loss of talent for the organization, "DoD's going to push it, and everyone is going to say, 'Roger that,' because that's their job. But inevitably what will happen is the same thing that people already do, they're going to vote with their feet." As John notes, integration may lead men in the organization to exit, which mirrored the survey results. Eighteen percent of men reported they would "definitely leave military service" if females were given the opportunity to serve in SF units and another 25 percent reported that they would be "likely to leave military service." The military is not alone in this respect. Many male-dominated professions have seen a perceived loss of prestige or exit of men as women have integrated. However, the military in general and SF in particular are unique in that there is no ready alternative organization that men can transition to where women will be excluded.

5 Conclusion

> The challenge initially, inevitably will be that integration with a male-dominated exclusive unit, because that's where their pride comes from. It's an exclusive club. Women aren't allowed, and it will degrade to them the meaning of Special Forces once women are welcomed into the branch.
>
> (Nicole, Participant)

Nicole discusses integration as a change that is going to happen, but one that men in SF will resist. Her comment hints at embedded stereotypes about women, that their mere presence makes an organization seem lesser. Throughout this Element, we have argued that resistance to gender integration and equity is present at the individual, cultural, and institutional levels and one unique form of this resistance is organizational obliviousness.

Organizational obliviousness refers to the intangible ways that stereotypes influence the everyday practices of the individual and the organization. The power of organizational obliviousness as a concept and organizational reality lies in its covert nature. Stereotypes, which may be based on gender, race, or other identity factors, are foundational to organizational obliviousness and operate at multiple levels in the organization. Grounded in the results of our data, we have focused on the pervasiveness of gender stereotyping at the individual, cultural, and institutional levels. Table 2 summarizes the ways organizational obliviousness plays out at each level of the organization and presents potential ways to address each of these levels.

At the individual level, organizational obliviousness occurs when gender stereotypes are used in everyday engagement between colleagues. Individual soldiers may not overtly express their biases, but they manifest in the workplace. Men are presented as the ideal soldier and women are othered and seen as outsiders. Gender is often understood as a static identity, which normalizes stereotyping as a part of the regular discourse in the organization. To address

Table 2 Level of organizational obliviousness

Level of Resistance	Example	Potential Organizational Response
Individual	Gender stereotypes used in everyday discussions and decision making	Military-specific training Outside experts Communities of support
Cultural	Women held up as tokens or the missteps of one applying to all; confirmation bias	Targeting leadership to set the tone and fostering networks of support
Institutional	Gendered policy and norms	Reviewing regulations and practices; adopting policies that shape norms to remove barriers of gender discrimination

this, the organization may bring in outside experts to facilitate implicit bias training and help uncover the covert ways that stereotypes show up. Bringing awareness to normalized stereotypes and the way they shape individual experiences is a first step to ensure they are not reinforced at the cultural level of the organization.

Stereotypes do covertly shape the norms of the organization, influencing the day-to-day practices of teams. At a cultural level, women are often held up as tokens, or the perceived missteps of one woman are held up as "evidence" that no woman can handle the environment. The military is constructed as a masculine organization where women are used as an example to illuminate what a soldier is not. The masculine culture is a point of pride, and women disrupt this ideal. Women entering the organization change a culture that current men in the organization believe works well. The gendered logics shape how people engage with the workplace, ensuring everyone knows how to behave within the male norms defined by gender stereotypes. To address this, leadership in the organization can set the tone of how integration should be implemented. Rather than focusing on the disruptions that women bring to the culture, or how they do not fit the prevailing norms, leaders may instead stress the benefits of integration and organizational change. Integration means that boundaries will shift regarding who is seen as an insider and outsider, and leaders must be prepared to navigate these changes without tokenizing women. Providing visibility to the gendered logic of the organization, and actively pushing back on it, is a step in shifting to a more equitable culture.

Finally, at the institutional level, organizational obliviousness often emerges in the ways gender is infused throughout norms and the implementation of policies. Policies reify norms and prevailing practices, reinforcing organizational inequities through ostensibly "objective" or neutral rules. Even as rules or policies are presented as neutral, they are often interpreted and implemented in gendered ways. Addressing this level of organizational obliviousness will require leaders to review policies and practices to ensure that they are written and carried out in ways that reinforce equity. The multilevel resistance to equity aided by organizational obliviousness requires a multilevel response. Rescinding the policy that denies women access to the opportunities is not enough; the military must consider how it addresses integration at each level of the organization.

Using both qualitative and quantitative data from one of the largest public organizations in the United States, throughout this Element we have unpacked how organizational obliviousness reinforces the multilevel resistance to women's integration. This adds to current discussions around gendered organizations and gender equity within public organizations. However, organizational obliviousness as a concept goes further than considering the gendered nature of organizations to show how stereotypes based on sociodemographic identities become covertly infused throughout organizations. Revealing how stereotypes covertly impact individuals, cultures, and institutional practices and policies brings us closer to understanding how we might achieve equity within public organizations.

References

Acker, J. (1990). Hierarchies, jobs, bodies: A theory of gendered organizations. *Gender & Society*, **4**(2), 139–158.

Acker, J. (2006). Inequality regimes: Gender, class, and race in organizations. *Gender & society*, **20**(4), 441–464.

Albert, S., & Whetten, D. A. (1985). Organizational identity. *Research in Organizational Behavior*, **7**, 263–295.

Alison, M. (2004). Women as agents of political violence: Gendering security. *Security Dialogue*, **35**(4), 447–463.

Asencio, M. (2002). *Sex and sexuality among New York's Puerto Rican youth*. Boulder: Lynne Rienner Publishers.

Bird, S. R. (2003). Sex composition, masculinity stereotype dissimilarity and the quality of men's workplace social relations. *Gender, Work and Organization*, 10(5), 579–604.

Bonilla-Silva, E. (2006). *Racism without racists: Color-blind racism and the persistence of racial inequality in the United States*. Lanham, MD: Rowman & Littlefield Publishers.

Bonilla-Silva, E., & Dietrich, D. (2011). The sweet enchantment of color-blind racism in Obamerica. *The Annals of the American Academy*, 634, 190–206.

Britton, D. M. (1997). Gendered organizational logic: Policy and practice in men's and women's prisons. *Gender & Society*, 11(6), 796–818.

Britton, D. M. (2000). The epistemology of the gendered organization. *Gender & Society*, **14**(3), 418–434.

Britton, D. M. (2003). *At work in the iron cage: The prison as gendered organization*. New York: New York University Press.

Burrelli, D. F. (2013). Women in combat: Issues for Congress. Washington, DC: Library of Congress, Congressional Research Service.

Butler, J. (1990). *Gender trouble and the subversion of identity*. New York: Routledge.

Charmaz, K. 2006. *Constructing grounded theory: A practical guide through qualitative analysis*. Thousand Oaks, CA: Sage Press.

Chatterjee, R. (2018). "A New Survey Finds 81 Percent of Women Have Experienced Sexual Harassment." *National Public Radio*. www.npr.org/sec tions/thetwo-way/2018/02/21/587671849/a-new-survey-finds-eighty-percent-of-women-have-experienced-sexual-harassment.

Chemaly, S. (2015). "Biology Doesn't Write Laws: Hillary Clinton's Bathroom Break Wasn't as Trivial as Some Might Like to Think." [Blog] *Huffington*

Post. www.huffingtonpost.com/soraya-chemaly/biology-doesnt-write-laws
_b_8874638.html.

Cohn, C. (2000). "How can she claim equal rights when she doesn't have to do as many push up as I do?" The framing of men's opposition to women's equality in the military. *Men & Masculinities*, **3**(2), 131–151.

Connell, R. (2006). Glass ceilings or gendered institutions? Mapping the gender regimes of public sector worksites. *Public Administration Review*, **66**(6), 837–849.

Courdileone, K. A. (2005). *Manhood and American political culture in the Cold War*. New York: Routledge.

Department of Defense. 2017. "Department of Defense Annual Report on Sexual Assault in the Military." http://sapr.mil/public/docs/reports/FY16_Annual/FY16_SAPRO_Annual_Report.pdf

Devilbiss, M. C. (1990). *Women and military service: A history, analysis, and overview of key issues*. Collingdale, PA: DIANE Publishing.

Doan, A. E., & Williams, J. C. (2008). The politics of virginity: Abstinence in sex education. *Social Forces*, **89**, 3.

Dolan, J. (2004). Gender equity: Illusion or reality for women in the federal executive service? *Public Administration Review*, 63(3), 299–308.

Dolan, J. (2000). The senior executive service: Gender, attitudes, and representative bureaucracy. *Journal of Public Administration Research and Theory*, **10**(3), 513–530.

Dull, M. (2010). Leadership and organizational culture: Sustaining dialogue between practitioners and scholars. *Public Administration Review*, **70**(6), 857–866.

Elshtain, J. B. (1995). *Women and war*. Chicago: University of Chicago Press.

Enloe, C. (2000). *Maneuvers: The international politics of militarizing women's lives*. Berkeley: University of California Press.

Fausto-Sterling, A. (1992). Building two-way streets: The case of feminism and science. *Nwsa Journal*, **4**(3), 336–349.

Fuegen, K., & Biernat, M. (2002). Reexamining the effects of solo status for women and men. *Personality and Social Psychology Bulletin*, 28(7), 913–925.

Gagliardi, P. (1986). The creation and change of organizational cultures: A conceptual framework. *Organization Studies*, **7**(2), 117–134.

Gioia, D. A., Schultz, M., & Corley, K. G. (2000). Organizational identity, image, and adaptive instability. *Academy of Management Review*, 25(1), 63–81.

Goldenhar, L. M., Swanson, N. G., Hurrell Jr., J. J., Ruder, A., & Deddens, J. (1998). Stressors and adverse outcomes for female construction workers. *Journal of Occupational Health Psychology*, 3(1), 19.

Hatch, M. (1993). The dynamics of organizational culture. *The Academy of Management Review*, 18(4), 657–693.

Herbert, M. S. (2000). *Camouflage isn't only for combat: Gender, sexuality, and women in the military*. New York: New York University Press.

Hesse-Biber, S. N., & Johnson, B. (2015). *The Oxford handbook of multimethod and mixed methods research inquiry*. Oxford: Oxford University Press.

Hinojosa, R. (2010). Doing hegemony: Military, men, and constructing a hegemonic masculinity. *Journal of Men's Studies*, 30, 179–194.

Hulett, D. M., Bendick Jr., M., Thomas, S. Y., & Moccio,F. (2008). Enhancing women's inclusion in firefighting in the USA. *International Journal of Diversity in Organisations, Communities & Nations*, 8(2), 189–207.

Jolls, C., & Sunstein, C. R. (2006). The law of implicit bias. *California Law Review*, 94, 969.

Jurik, N. C. (1985). Individual and organizational determinants of correctional officer attitudes toward inmates. *Criminology*, 23(3), 523–540.

Jurik, N. C. (1988). Striking a balance: Female correctional officers, gender role stereotypes, and male prisons. *Sociological Inquiry*, 58(3), 291–305

Kanter, R. M. (1977). Some effects of proportions on group life: Skewed sex ratios and responses to token women. *American journal of Sociology*, 82(5), 965–990.

Kanter, R.M. (2008). *Men and women of the corporation: New edition*. New York: Basic Books.

Keenan, J. O. (2008). The DoD combat exclusion policy: Time for a change? In M. M. Putko & D. V. Johnson (Eds.), *Women in combat compendium* (pp. 21–25). Washington, DC: Strategic Studies Institute. http://wiisglobal.org/wpcontent/uploads/2013/05/Women-in-Combat-Compendium1.pdf.

Keiser, L. R., Wilkins, V. M., Meier, K. J., & Holland, C. A. (2002). Lipstick and logarithms: Gender, institutional context, and representative bureaucracy. *American Political Science Review*, 96(3), 553–564.

Kimmel, M. (2000). Saving the males: The sociological implications of the Virginia Military Institute and the Citadel. *Gender & Society*, 14(4), 494–516.

Kotter, J. P., & Heskett, J. L. (2011). *Corporate culture and performance*. New York: Free Press.

Kuipers, B. S., Higgs, M., Kickert, W., Tummers, L., Grandia, J., & Van der Voet, J. (2014). The management of change in public organizations: A literature review. *Public Administration*, 92(1), 1–20.

Kumar, S., & Kant, S., 2006. Organizational resistance to participatory approaches in public agencies: An analysis of forest department's resistance to community-based forest management. *International Public Management Journal*, 9(2), 141–173.

Lewis, P., & Simpson, R. (Eds.). (2010). *Revealing and concealing gender: Issues of visibility in organizations.* Berlin: Springer.

Lewis, P., & Simpson, R. (2012). Kanter revisited: Gender, power and (in) visibility. *International Journal of Management Reviews,* 14(2), 141–158.

Linskey, A. (2015) "In swing states, Clinton may face gender bias. Voters often reluctant to back female candidates," *The Boston Globe.* www.bostonglobe.com/news/nation/2015/09/09/hillary-clinton-faces-challenges-unique-woman-running-for-office/Zkv99eyLTzAVzskuGnvRPN/story.html

MacKenzie, M. (2015). *Beyond the band of brothers.* Cambridge: Cambridge University Press.

Martin, S. E., & Jurik, N. (2007). *Doing justice, doing gender: Women in legal and criminal justice occupations,* 2nd ed. Thousand Oaks, CA: Sage Publications.

Morden, B. J. (1990). *The women's Army corps, 1945–1978.* Washington, DC: Center of Military History, United States Army.

Nagel, J., & Feitz, L. 2007. Deploying race, gender, class, and sexuality in the Iraq War. *Race, Gender & Class,* 14(3–4), 28–47.

O'Leary, R. (2014). *The ethics of dissent: Managing guerrilla government.* Los Angeles: SAGE.

O'Reilly, C., & Chatman, J. (1996). Culture as social control: Corporations, cults, and commitment. In B. M. Staw & L. L. Cummings (Eds.), *Research in organizational behaviour: An annual series of analytical essays and critical reviews.* Vol. 18, pp. 157–200. Atlanta: Elsevier Science/JAI Press.

Owen, D., & Dennis, J. (1988). Gender differences in the politicization of American children. *Women & Politics,* 8(2), 23–43.

Parashar, S. (2009). Feminist international relations and women militants: Case studies from Sri Lanka and Kashmir. *Cambridge Review of International Affairs,* 22(2), 235–256.

Patten, E., & Parker, K. (2011). Women in the US military: Growing share, distinctive profile. Washington, DC: Pew Research Center. www.pewsocial trends.org/2011/12/22/women-in-the-u-s-military-growing-share-distinctive-profile/

Penner, Barbara. (2012). "We shall deal here with humble things." *Places Journal.* https://placesjournal.org/article/we-shall-deal-here-with-humble-things/.

Petersen, T., & Morgan, L. A. (1995). Separate and unequal: Occupation-establishment sex segregation and the gender wage gap. *American Journal of Sociology,* 101(2), 329–365.

Pettigrew, A. M., Woodman, R. W., & Cameron, K. S. (2001). Studying organizational change and development: Challenges for future research. *Academy of Management Journal*, 44(4), 697–713.

Piderit, S. K. (2000). Rethinking resistance and recognizing ambivalence: A multidimensional view of attitudes toward an organizational change. *Academy of Management Review*, 25(4), 783–794.

Portillo, S. (2010) How race, sex, and age frame use of authority by local government officials. *Law and Social Inquiry*, 35(3), 603–623.

Powell, W. W., & DiMaggio, P. J. (Eds.). (2012). *The new institutionalism in organizational analysis*. Chicago: University of Chicago Press.

Plaskow, J. (2008). Embodiment, elimination, and the role of toilets in struggles for social justice. *CrossCurrents*, 58(1), 51–64.

Prokos, A., & Padavic, I. (2002). "There oughtta be a law against bitches": Masculinity lessons in police academy training. *Gender, Work & Organization*, 9(4), 439–459.

Ridgeway, C. L. (1997). Interaction and the conservation of gender inequality: Considering employment. *American Sociological Review*, 62(2), 218–235.

Sabharwal, M. (2015). From glass ceiling to glass cliff: Women in senior executive service. *Journal of Public Administration Research and Theory*, 25(2), 399–426.

Saidel, J. R., & Loscocco, K. (2005). Agency leaders, gendered institutions, and representative bureaucracy. *Public Administration Review*, 65(2), 158–170.

Santangelo, S. (2014, March 28). Fourteen women have tried, and failed, the Marines' Infantry Officer Course: Here's why. *The Washington Post*. www .washingtonpost.com/opinions/fourteen-women-have-tried-and-failed-the -marines-infantry-officer-course-heres-why/2014/03/28/24a83ea0-b145- 11e3-a49e-76adc9210f19_story.html.

Sasson-Levy, O. (2003). Feminism and military gender practices: Israeli women soldiers in "masculine" roles. *Sociological Inquiry*, 73(3), 440–465.

Schein, E. H. (1984). Coming to a new awareness of organizational culture. *Sloan Management Review*, 25(2), 3–16.

Schein, E. H. (1990). Organizational culture. *American Psychological Association*, 45(2), 109.

Schein, E. H. (2010). *Organizational culture and leadership*. San Francisco: Jossey-Bass.

SHARP (2018) "What we know about sexual assault of military men." Sexual Harassment/Assault Response & Prevention. www.sexualassault.army.mil /whatweknow_militarymen.aspx

Skaine, R. (1999). *Women at war: Gender issues of Americans in combat*. Jefferson, NC:McFarland & Company.

Stack-O'Connor, A. (2007). Lions, tiger, and freedom birds: How and why Liberation Tigers of Tamil employs women. *Terrorism and Political Violence*, 19(1), 43–63.

Tinkler, J. (2012). Resisting the enforcement of sexual harassment law. *Law & Social Inquiry*, 37(1), 1–24.

Tinker, J. (2008). "People are too quick to take offense": The effects of legal information and beliefs on definitions of sexual harassment. *Law & Social Inquiry* 33(2), 417–445.

Tinkler, J., LI, Y.E., & Mollborn, S. (2007). Can legal interventions change beliefs? The effect of exposure to sexual harassment policy on men's gender beliefs. *Social Psychology Quarterly*, 70(4), 480–494.

Voorhees, H., & Skaggs, R.L.-S. (2015). Women leading government: Why so little progress in 30 years? *Public Management*, **97**(1), 6–10, 12–13.

Zimmer, L. (1988). Tokenism and women in the workplace: The limits of gender-neutral theory. *Social Problems*, **35**(1), 64–77.

Cambridge Elements ☰

Public and Nonprofit Administration

Andrew Whitford

University of Georgia

Andrew Whitford is Alexander M. Crenshaw Professor of Public Policy in the School of Public and International Affairs at the University of Georgia. His research centers on strategy and innovation in public policy and organization studies.

Robert Christensen

Brigham Young University

Robert Christensen specializes in nonprofit and public management. He is Division Chair for the Public and Nonprofit Division at the Academy of Management, and serves as an elected member of the Public Management Research Association board.

About the Series

The foundation of this series are cutting-edge contributions on emerging topics and definitive reviews of keystone topics in public and nonprofit administration, especially those that lack longer treatment in textbook or other formats. Among keystone topics of interest for scholars and practitioners of public and nonprofit administration, it covers public management, public budgeting and finance, nonprofit studies, and the interstitial space between the public and nonprofit sectors, along with theoretical and methodological contributions, including quantitative, qualitative and mixed-methods pieces.

The Public Management Research Association

The Public Management Research Association improves public governance by advancing research on public organizations, strengthening links among interdisciplinary scholars, and furthering professional and academic opportunities in public management.

Cambridge Elements ≡

Public and Nonprofit Administration

Elements in the Series

Motivating Public Employees
Marc Esteve and Christian Schuster

Organizational Obliviousness: Entrenched Resistance to Gender Integration in the Military
Alesha Doan and Shannon Portillo

A full series listing is available at: www.cambridge.org/EPNP

Printed in the United States
By Bookmasters